Picking Up The Pieces

A Guide to Recovery from Betrayal and a Broken Heart

by

Dinah S. Temple

First published by AuthorHouse 08/23/04

ISBN: 1-4184-5900-3 (e-book)
ISBN: 1-4184-4047-7 (Paperback)

This book is printed on acid free paper.

This book is available at a quantity
discount directly from AuthorHouse
at
www.authorhouse.com/bookstore/itemdetail.aspx?bookid=19983

DEDICATION

To my ex, who masqueraded as the love of my life.

I want to thank you. If not for the devastating way you walked out of my life, I never would have written this book. You have motivated me to help others through the same pain I suffered, and doing so rewards me more than you can imagine.

I have a brand new, wonderful life and my once broken heart is happy and whole again.

SPECIAL THANKS

Thanks to my sister-in-law Toni for holding my hand through it all. Your love and support meant everything.

Thanks to my best friend Mary. You have always been there for me and I thank you for that. I know I can always count on you no matter what.

Thanks to my son Kevin. You saw me at my worst and lived with me through the lowest point of my life. I hope you can be proud of the woman who emerged from the darkness. Thanks for putting up with me honey. I love you always.

Thanks to my brother Daryl and my sister-in-law Tami. This book represents so much more than I expected because of you.

Thanks to my family. You allowed me to grieve and recover without interference or judgment. I needed that.

Thanks to my mom, for showing me how to be a survivor. Everything I know, I learned from you.

CONTENTS

INTRODUCTION

I know you probably never thought you would be reading a self-help book like this one. Believe me, I never thought in a million years I'd be writing one. Just a short time ago, I took great comfort in believing that this, my second marriage, would last forever and that I would never again have to be single.

A month after my husband left, I found myself in the book section of a local store, looking for a self-help book, preferably one entitled *How to Mend a Broken Heart*. I had no luck in my search for self-help that day. Instead, in that moment, I experienced a profound revelation about myself—an epiphany of sorts. That is, what I wanted most desperately in my life was to be the permanent other half of someone's heart. This spiritual security was something I had sadly taken for granted.

I also realized that while I had been tucked securely in my marriage with a seemingly perfect husband and our perfect love, I never dreamed I could feel such devastation. Suddenly I was lost, no longer part of a couple. I was just a single mom again, now with a teenager to raise.

I asked myself, "How did I get to this point"? There I stood, mourning a dead marriage that only a few, short months before had been alive and happy. I had seen no signs of what was to come. Even worse, I was still desperately in love with my husband, believing in the perfect love we had shared.

For the next several months I struggled against my desire to fan the fires of that love and the necessity of just getting up everyday, going through life just trying to remember to breathe.

I'm sure that many women and men are searching for the same answers I needed. You are probably reading this book in an effort to come to grips with the reality of what has happened to you. You may have the sense that your situation doesn't feel real or permanent yet. You are seeking answers while your broken heart bleeds all over the floor, and all you want right now is for someone to show you how to make the pain stop.

I'm sorry to tell you that no one can do that for you. Only *you* can make it stop hurting. I learned this through months of soul searching and by asking myself tough questions about my experience. In doing so, I gained a much better understanding of relationships and myself as well as how to be happy again.

I hope that by reading my book you will learn the methods I used to get through my loss. Perhaps by doing as I did, you will find new life and new love. You will see that you too can pick up the pieces of your broken heart and make it want to beat again. You *can* process the pain and gain an understanding of why your heart got broken in the first place. You *can* learn how to heal your heart and your spirit. You *can* learn to rebuild your life and be happy again. And you *can* love again.

Throughout this book, I will tell you my story and how I became a survivor of betrayal and heartbreak. Hopefully, you can use my personal journey of pain and recovery as a benchmark for your own. I intend to guide you through the pain and show you how I accomplished what I never thought I could. I learned how to recover and regain my self-esteem as well as how to repair my broken spirit. In the process, I rediscovered the wonderful happy person I used to be before the breakup.

Above all, know that you are not alone in your heartbreak. You *will* get through the dark tunnel of pain and your heart *will* heal. I will show you how to rebuild your life and be happy again. Keep reading and see yourself throughout my story, experiencing pain like yours. You will find your way back.

Good luck on this journey. It is your personal quest for your spirit. Once found, your spirit will carry you the rest of the way.

x

1

Process It

Admitting the reality of your loss is the first step on a journey of discovery and recovery. Though painful, this acknowledgement will allow you to begin the healing process.

If you believe in commitment and fidelity as I do, you probably thought your marriage or relationship would last forever. I thought that a love as deep as ours could withstand any obstacle, and together, my husband and I could overcome anything. After all, hadn't we promised each other to be faithful, to grow old together, to be best friends, to care for one another with love, honor and respect until death?

We had made plans and shared dreams. We were two people in love who always got along. In fact, in the two years we were together, my husband and I never fought.

1

The few minor disagreements we had were discussed and amicable solutions were reached. No muss, no fuss.

So why did the love of my life leave? It's likely you are asking yourself the same question. Just as I did, you may be second-guessing your previous life. It took about two and a half months before I realized that my marriage was over. In that two and a half-month period, I put my relationship under a microscope, analyzing every conversation, every happy memory, everything we shared. I was trying to see if I missed the signs of a marriage breaking up. Guess what? There were no signs. I started questioning why then did my marriage fail? I asked myself if what we had was real? Did he ever really love me? Did he leave because I'm not young enough or attractive enough? Was it my personality? Was there something I could have done to prevent our breakup? How could I love someone so much and be so wrong about him?

I encourage you to answer each of your own haunting questions to your satisfaction. I found that, in my case, doing so was the only way I could move forward.

In examining *my* marriage and facing my own answers to the tough questions, I looked inward and I found that I *had* sincerely tried to be the perfect wife and person I knew how to be. And you know what? Realizing that made me feel better. I didn't just *love* him; I was *in love* with him. I would have done absolutely anything for him. I supported him emotionally and was always there when he needed me. I gave him the freedom to do whatever he wanted—as long as it made him happy.

I have a good job, I work hard, and I love with all that I am. I am attractive, intelligent, funny, sexy and fun to be with. As a couple, the two of us always had a great time, no matter what we were doing. We always held hands and kissed to the point that everyone we knew wanted what we had. We agreed on most things and even when we didn't, it was never a big deal. We were very happy and told each other so, often.

So when I asked myself, finally, if he left because of who I am, the answer had to be *no*. In fact, all my answers led to only one conclusion—that is, if I had it to do over again, I would change only one thing, and that would be more communication.

In retrospect, I can see now that we were not meant to be together. I know this because my husband was obviously not happy and being happy with me would have required one or both of us to change who we are. Make no mistake. If you have to change yourself to please someone else, or vice versa, then you are with the wrong person.

One cannot go through life, successfully happy, if they have to walk on eggshells and pretend to be something they're not or feel something they don't. If your relationship ended, it's likely because you were with the wrong person in the first place. I truly believe that the RIGHT person does not walk away. The RIGHT person stays to work problems out and will do whatever it takes to make the relationship work.

It took a while but I realized that some people don't know when they have a good thing. They always want better. Sadly, they usually find out too late that the grass isn't greener; it is only different.

I also have to believe that things happen for a reason and I can only hope that next time, I will love someone mature enough to have learned this hard lesson. I hope he will be someone who will love and honor me as I was meant to be. At the same time, I intend to remember that there are no guarantees in life or in love, and I will cherish each moment as if it were my last.

You will draw *your* own conclusions when you are able to honestly answer questions about your failed relationship.

2

My Fairy Tale Love

Three weeks after I met my husband, I was head over heels in love. Both of us were, in fact. Our time together was magic. We couldn't keep our hands off of each other and spent every waking moment together. It was as if our hearts were magnets.

We talked at length about everything under the sun because we wanted to know so much about each other. I just *knew* he was THE ONE. I knew even in this short period of time, especially after having been in a ten-year previous marriage and other relationships, which turned sour. This was the man I was born to be with.

At the time, he had a job that paid about $10 an hour and lived rent-free in a run-down, bug-infested house owned by his boss. In exchange for the free rent, he provided after-hours security for the commercial lot. He wasn't happy there, though. He felt underpaid and got no respect from those he worked with. Soon after we met, he decided to look elsewhere for a job. Finding one, he quit his current job, leaving him with no place to live.

I was only too happy to offer him my home since he was there every night after work anyway. And he gratefully accepted my invitation. From that moment on, he gave me the majority of his paycheck every week. Three months later, we were married on a beautiful sunny day in Sandbridge, Virginia. We said our vows as the water washed up to the shore and over our bare feet. It was the happiest day of our lives.

A year later, I helped him get a civil service job with the government. Applying for a job with the government is more difficult than most people realize. I typed up his resume, helped him prepare the government application and then made sure it got to the appropriate place before the deadline. Whatever he needed or wanted, I was there for him. Whether it was my presence at a fishing tournament in March or just picking up his dry cleaning, I was happy to do it.

I loved doing little things for my husband as well. I got up an hour earlier than I had to everyday just to have the chance to talk with him a few minutes before he left for work. I made sure he got his coffee, a packed lunch, and a loving kiss good-bye. I kept a mental note of everything he wanted and needed, no matter how seemingly insignificant. We could always provide the little things we wanted for each other, but larger items, like lifts for his truck and a high-tech printer for me, took a bit longer to get. We saved the money and, little by little, we would get something we needed and wanted.

It was always my plan to make sure he got everything he wanted eventually. I loved him so much that I would have given him the world if I could have.

My husband told me more than once that I had saved his life. He said I threw him a lifeline. Looking back, I see that it's true. I dreamt his dreams with him. I loved him for himself, not for any material thing he could offer me. Everything I ever did for him I would do again.

I loved being married to this man. I adored him for treating me with respect and for making me feel safe and loved. He left roses on my windshield at work on unofficial

anniversaries. Flowers were always waiting for me at home
if he knew I had had a rough day.

He put a shawl around my shoulders anytime he
thought I might be cold, and he always knew when
anything was bothering me and encouraged me to talk
about it. He was my biggest fan, my best friend and lover.
He came home to me every night. He held my hand when
we went anywhere, even when we were just watching TV.
We always sat so close together on the couch that no light
could shine between us.

He kissed and hugged me goodbye every morning
and greeted me with a big hug and kiss every night when
I arrived home. Come to think of it, he would even kiss
me before he would go out to check the mail and while
standing in line at a grocery store. We both lived for the
affection. A co-worker of his once told me that my husband
talked about me like I was Christmas. My husband loved
Christmas, so this comment meant a lot to me.

During the days or weeks we spent apart because of his
National Guard reservist duties, I would carry the phone
around with me, even to the bathroom, just to make sure
I didn't miss his call. I would also sit on our front porch,

minutes before he was due to arrive home. I watched for his truck to turn the corner because I couldn't wait to see him. Some might call that pathetic. I called it love.

Unfortunately, it was love from a heart soon to be shattered by the very man I trusted most in this world. Be careful with love that plays out like a fairy tale. If it seems too good to be true, it usually is. More times than not, fairy tale love tends to hasten to the part of the story we all hate to hear….THE END.

3

Why They Walk Away

You're probably wondering how such a love could break down. I agonized over the question, "So why doesn't he still love me"? Everyone we knew envied our relationship and wanted a love like ours. I had felt secure in a love meant to last forever and was now left alone and utterly betrayed.

Thus began several months of painful reflection, which ultimately led to my drawing several conclusions about myself, my husband, and some relationships in general. In studying why my husband left me, I concluded that certain people leave great relationships for many reasons, most of them universal in nature. Aside from the obvious reasons like irreconcilable differences and fighting over finances, there are a few other reasons that stand out. I will illustrate the reasons by defining the different groups of people who walk away. You may see your loved one in my analysis.

Fantasy Seekers

We've all met them. You know the folks that have no concept of what real life is all about. These people are unable to make the normal transition from dating to a settled relationship.

They envision a good relationship as more of a fantasy to be fulfilled than as a real work in progress. They are stuck in that dating phase where everything is pretty… romantic…sexy…and fun. Unfortunately, as much as we may want to live in this world full-time, the reality is that sooner or later we have to leave the pink cloud, settle in and make sure that the day-to-day needs of life are met. The bills have to be paid, the kids are going to bicker, and occasionally, someone will lose a job and so on. The Fantasy Seekers simply move on when the going gets tough. We shouldn't expect life to be perfect, only the best we can make it. Those who expect the former can be disappointed when mundane realities of life disturb their impossibly fantasized perceptions. Fantasy Seekers also tend to be quite insecure and because of that, when put in a vulnerable situation, are left open to temptation and flattery from the opposite sex. They enjoy feeling attractive and desirable to someone other than their spouse. It's exciting at first to them because, again, they can experience the feeling of the dating phase just by flirting with someone else. Unfortunately, before they know it, sometimes "harmless flirting" takes a serious wrong turn.

This type of love is up for sale to the highest bidder and the spouse is not allowed to bid or to even know there is an auction in progress. The inability to be satisfied with the daily matters of life that go along with any relationship is a serious failing. These people just want to have fun. If any work or compromise is involved in keeping a relationship together, they're out of there.

And so, an affair begins and continues until **that** relationship begins to require work and then these folks will move on again. I can only conclude that in my husband's eyes, I just didn't measure up anymore. He lost sight of the person he fell in love with. He had placed me on a pedestal, and his girlfriend managed to shove me off. Sadly, he failed to break my fall and just stood by to watch the descent.

As painful as that realization was, I have come to accept it. My feet are now planted firmly on the ground. I know that if *I* didn't measure up, no one else can ever come close. It was his fantasy, and it is *his* loss. Remember that and make it your mantra.

The Wave Riders

The Wave Riders are the folks who are along for a good and thrilling ride and then, when the ride is over, so are they.

These folks lack the ability to recognize a good thing when they have it. In fact, they place very little value on relationships unless there is something in it for them— always, all the time. In short, this is the classic case of becoming bored with a relationship. The Wave Rider forgets all of the qualities in you and your relationship that made him or her fall in love in the first place because the excitement of the ride is over. Of course, the Wave Rider makes no attempt to create any excitement on his or her own. Often the reason a person leaves is not what's lacking in you. It's what is lacking in *him* or *her.*

To use an analogy, think of someone being lost in the desert. Just when he feels he's going to die, he sees a clear spring far off in the distance, seemingly out of reach. Water! Not only does he want the water, he needs it for his survival. He is willing to do anything to get it, and he finally works his way to the spring.

The first drink fills him with the joy that he is not going to die. The next gallon satisfies his need for water. At this point, he needs water only on a regular basis throughout his daily life. After a time in the oasis, he realizes he can get water anytime and begins to take it for granted.

Likewise, after working hard for that lifelong relationship, some people become too comfortable and begin to take their love for granted. I believe the reason for this is that some people have a distorted view of what a relationship is and how it should be incorporated into daily life. He or she may think that if they have to make small compromises along the way (if they find out you don't have the same taste in movies or television, for instance), the two of you must not be a good match.

He or she may believe there is a perfect person out there who is a mirror image of themselves, and go looking

17

for them. They may even find a person who shares some of their likes and dislikes; however, ultimately, this person probably lacks many other characteristics deemed essential in a good mate. The error in judgment can seem obvious to everyone but him or her.

In short, someone who is blind to the good in his partner needs to get a grip on the reality of how a strong, loving relationship really works and lasts. Even though a relationship may seem so sweet and strong, the one who leaves may lack the ability to maintain that focus and, therefore, fails to make the love between you last.

The Takers

These people have no concept of what happiness is or how to achieve it. In fact, they believe happiness is a gift owed to them by someone else.

There is a big difference in the statements "he makes me happy" and "I am happy with him". The Takers don't realize that we are not put on this earth to make others happy. Giving someone joy is not our duty, nor is it within our abilities. Happiness is only the feeling generated or achieved by someone for his or her own sake.

We must be happy with ourselves first and because of that, others will be happy with us, not because of us. The fact is, no one can actually make happiness for someone else. Unfortunately, some people blame their state of unhappiness on their partner instead of placing the blame where it really lives.

The Superior Wanna Be's

Another reason some people leave is because they may feel inferior. Even though you may have loved your partner with all your heart, he or she may have found the need to be in control and superior to be stronger than the need to stay.

Many people seek out someone who, because of their physical appearance and personality, would feel inferior to them. This, therefore in their mind, makes them the superior one. My husband left me for someone whose physical characteristics are in direct contrast with those he always claimed to want in a woman. I can't help wondering if he feels superior now.

It's much easier for someone to feel secure if they also feel that their partner *lacks* that same security. Their partner is usually so grateful to be with them, they would do anything to keep that person. After all, what more could a person want than someone who obeys their every command and fulfills their every wish regardless of the consequences? A Superior Wanna Be is not looking for a partner with his or her own ideas and the backbone to speak them out loud, despite the possibility of resistance. This type of person requires compromise from their partners and this is something that insecure men and women avoid at all costs.

Chemical Effects of Love

On a more scientific note, when people fall in love, there actually is a chemical cocktail brewing in their brains. It is this beautiful mixture of PEA, Dopamine and Norepinephrine that produce a state of euphoria and blissful excitement. This is why new lovers seem to have more energy, can stay up all night talking or making love and experience the fluttering of butterflies in the stomach. The drug-like effects of PEA, Dopamine, and Norepinephrine are addictive. Unfortunately like any addiction, the body builds up a tolerance to these chemicals over time. New lovers then require more, at a higher dose to maintain the initial high they once felt.

Once the tolerance levels peak, the body begins to replace the euphoric producing neurochemicals with endorphins. Much like the painkiller morphine, endorphins reduce anxiety and cause feelings of well being and comfort. It is suspected that endorphins and the feelings they produce in couples are largely responsible for relationships lasting a lifetime. Fortunately, many accept the feelings of "settling in" as the natural progression from new love to lasting love.

On the other hand, documented studies report the theory that the euphoric effects of PEA, Dopamine, and Norepinephrine start to diminish somewhere between one to four years after a relationship begins. This is in direct correlation with when many relationships breakup. At this stage, partners are no longer seen through rose colored glasses. Many crave the elated feeling which new love produces and will leave a relationship in search of another fix.

The point is that people walk away for all kinds of reasons. Some are really minor and petty. Some are so serious that it's hard to overcome them. Once you process the fact that your relationship is really broken, the next step to recovery is to identify *why* it happened. If you don't understand why it happened, you can't avoid having the same situation happen again.

For those of you who have not reached this conclusion yet, you need to look at the Pyramid of Discovery and peel the onion back, as far it will go. To explain further, when you figure out why you think the relationship broke, keep asking why until the real and true answer is revealed. Continue until you are satisfied that you have arrived at the final answer you seek.

Pyramid of Discovery

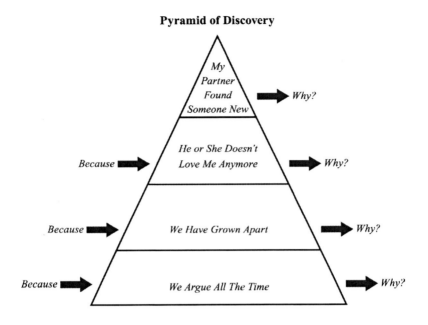

The last question you need to ask yourself is why you would want to hang on to this relationship. Accept the fact that you may not be able to change anything even after you do understand why. If you feel you are in fact to blame, you must forgive yourself and take steps to ensure the same mistakes are not repeated. If you feel your partner is the one to blame, you must find a way to forgive him or her too.

4

The Healing Process

How to Begin

First, you have to cry a lot. You must mourn your loss. Cry until no more tears will fall. Cry until you realize he or she is not worth one more tear.

Then, decide whether to live or die. Your spouse or partner is not worth dying over so that's not an option. Do not leave a wake of grief behind for loved ones who don't deserve it. One of you is worth ten thousand of him or her.

Next, get angry and decide how you will succeed despite it all. Your spirit is precious and it must be restored.

Finally, gain an understanding of what has happened and, most importantly, why. Until you can make sense of it, you will not be able to move forward.

Right now, you might feel broken, weak, pitiful and victimized. These are only natural feelings, but you must work toward becoming a strong, confident, self-reliant survivor. This outcome is what your children and your family would choose for you.

In fact, survival is your only option. Allow me to illustrate. Imagine that you are thrown out into the middle of the ocean with only a life jacket. You see land on the horizon and sharks coming up behind you. Do you swim for shore and give it all you've got, or do you surrender to the sharks?

There really isn't a choice to be made because only one decision makes sense. You must survive, and you will survive. Don't allow yourself to hesitate or doubt this fact. You must believe in yourself like never before. Sometimes, you are all you've got.

As you begin to heal, you must learn to be objective about yourself. Think how you would advise your sister, brother or best friend in the same situation. What would you tell *them* to do? You are worthy of the same good advice.

Nurture your heart but follow your head as you move forward to the place that is best for you. It may not be where you want to go right now. But, I promise, you'll be grateful you had the courage to survive.

Living in an Upside-down World

You need to allow yourself time to mourn the death of your relationship because, the fact is, what you had will never be the same again. At the end of your journey, you will be different and wiser. You will realize *there is life after loss*, but only after the journey's end. For now, your grief is ruling your mind and controlling your life.

After my husband left, I found myself in a tailspin. My whole world had turned upside-down in the blink of an eye. During this difficult time, I allowed the deep love I still felt for him to overshadow everything else in my life. In short, my love for him was destroying me.

I was unable to focus on what was most important, namely my son, my job and my own well being. As the only things left in my life, these were ultimately the reasons

I managed to get back on track. However, to ensure my success in this endeavor and to be on the safe side, I sought medical treatment in the form of anxiety medication. Doing this worked wonders on my thought processes. With the help of this mild prescription, I was finally able to concentrate, sleep, and begin healing.

If you have children, you are probably unaware of it, but they are saving your life right now. You see, children do not fully comprehend what has happened to you. Nor do they understand your change in mood, sleeping habits etc. To them, today is the same as any other day. Your children will continue to demand your attention just as they always have. Let's face it. For many of you, your children are the only reason you get up everyday. Without them, you might continue to wallow in your grief, spiraling yourself further and further downward.

You need to realize something about your grief. When someone mourns, several destructive behaviors tend to rear their ugly heads. These include deep depression, thoughts of suicide, self-blame, alcohol abuse, sleep deprivation, inability to focus and loss of appetite. It may surprise you to know that those behaviors are bi-products of grief and are 100% normal. In fact, if someone going through this trauma didn't exhibit some of these behaviors, someone would need to check their pulse! Not only are these behaviors normal and automatic but it is also something other people are powerless to change for you. You have to decide whether or not your lost partner is worth these feelings and worth living your life, upside-down.

Please identify your vulnerabilities as soon as possible and seek any assistance you may require.

Recovery

Recovering from a broken heart is much like recovering from a natural disaster. First, you must assess the damage. Then you discard what is irreparable and keep what can be salvaged. From there, you plan to rebuild. Only this time, you make sure the foundation and structure are storm proof. What you rebuild should be stronger than before.

Everyone mourns and recovers in their own way and in their own time. The hard part is that you must first go through the pain to get to the other side—recovery. Feel the pain, but don't let it control you. It's time to start taking your life back and you must protect yourself from anything that may come next.

When the love of my life left, I learned that I hadn't known him as well as I thought I did. I would have never guessed that he was unhappy or that he would leave our beautiful life. But the fact is, he did.

I recognized that though I still loved him, this time in my life had to be all about surviving my betrayal. I did whatever it took to protect myself, because no one else was going to do it for me. Here are ten steps I used to survive the breakup of my marriage.

Protect Yourself

After the fog cleared, I knew I could no longer trust my husband to do the right thing. So I shifted into self-preservation mode. I changed bank accounts and the locks. I canceled credit cards. Trying to be practical and cautious, I did whatever I could think to do to protect my self-interests.

Eliminate all Reminders of Your Partner

I had been separated from my husband about five weeks when our two-year anniversary rolled around. The pain was still so fresh that I couldn't even buy milk with the same expiration date as our anniversary. I knew I wouldn't be able to handle seeing that date staring me in the face every day until the milk was gone.

I began to clean house, so to speak, and removed everything in it that reminded me of him. Even if you think your separation may be only temporary, you would do well to remove any reminder of your ex from your house, workplace or car. What you don't need to return to your ex should be stored or thrown away. This includes your pictures, rings or jewelry, CDs, tapes or videos you bought together, computer games, files, etc. You get the idea. The sooner you feel single, the sooner you will find yourself and forget the pain.

I stored my collection in the attic, in a box labeled "PANDORA."

Reach Out for Support

During the most painful period of my recovery, I reached out to my friends and family and found an extremely effective support system. These people were my lifelines; they listened when I needed to talk (and I needed to talk often). You may be extremely lonely as I was. Do yourself a favor and surround yourself with positive individuals who are genuinely rooting for your recovery.

Set Specific, Attainable Goals

My breakup left me so completely and unexpectedly alone that I could not function as an individual for a time. I had forgotten how to be alone and happy. One way I fought the loneliness after the devastating first six weeks was by replacing the emptiness my husband left in my life. I did this by staying busy, by filling every minute of my day with something to do or focus on.

As I reflected on how I would begin again, I decided there were many things I wanted to accomplish to better my life. I began to set goals for myself and devise steps to take in order to reach those goals.

I cannot tell you how much making this decision changed my entire outlook on life without my husband. By filling every spare minute with planned projects, I began to heal myself by not wasting excess time wondering "what if". I know that my recovery would have taken a whole lot longer if I had not thrown myself into accomplishing positive things for myself.

I have met many of my goals already, and I must say the sense of satisfaction is great. You will find strength in setting and completing some of your own goals.

Keep a Journal

I decided to begin writing in a journal early on in my experience because it was such a release to get thoughts out of my head and down on paper. In a way, writing has saved me by allowing me to see things as they really are—in black and white.

I had questions that only my spouse could answer, and he wasn't talking. Seeing my thoughts in print helped me sort out and answer these questions myself. I reviewed our life together, writing it out in detail. Then I went over every past event and conversation that might reveal why he had left me.

Eventually I came to several insightful conclusions that allowed me to accept what had happened, decide how to deal with it, and move forward.

Finish a Joint Project

I began and finished a project my husband and I had planned to do together, which was to construct a new, larger shed for the backyard. I felt that in some small way, if I could complete this project on my own, it would stand as a statement to myself and to him that I didn't need him anymore. Its effect was indeed therapeutic. I also continued to garden, and did other home improvements that he started and never finished.

Pursue New Interests

I took up many hobbies—projects that challenged me to be creative. I surprised myself with what I could achieve, and every little thing I pursued took my mind off him.

I got into a self-improvement frenzy, changing my hairstyle and doing a lot of other things to improve the way I felt about myself. I also checked into plastic surgery, something I had always wanted to do. I bought exercise equipment, went on vacation to the beach, took walks, and went out with friends.

I began to visit Internet chat rooms, reading comments from others like me. I came away with some good advice and a better understanding of how often someone is left by a spouse under the same circumstances.

I also went out to clubs, not so much to start a new relationship, but to be around people and make new friends, both male and female. Making new friends is a positive step. Just as you enrich their lives, they will enrich yours. I discovered that men were still drawn to me as I hoped they would be. Men in the age range of 22 to 35 began asking me out. I was 43. Talk about a real ego boost! Still, I didn't accept any dates until the divorce papers were signed. It took me almost a year to be comfortable with dating again.

Think about developing a new hobby for yourself, or dust off an old one. Healing takes time and right now you have too much time on your hands. Fill the void with something you love to do. Better yet, see if money can be made from it. You will feel better, I promise.

By engaging *my* mind in active pursuits, I was able to change my thinking and my attitude. I began to feel more like my old self—my pre-marriage, independent, strong, surviving self. And I began to feel that I was going to be OK.

Restore Your Spirit

As you search for new interests in your life, you must not forget to recover your spirit along the way.

You remember your spirit, don't you? It's the twinkle in your eye, the spark in your heart, the tears, the laughter, the dreamer in you. It's your happiness, your strength, and your right from wrong. It's the trust in yourself, your ideals and morals, the smile on others' faces when you're near them. It's your joy, the triumph you achieve when life presents bumps in the road. Your spirit is what everyone misses about you when you're not around.

Many people are able to make great contributions to the world and to humanity through their generosity of spirit. Most of us, though, don't have the resources and live on a much less grand scale. Instead, we contribute in small ways like our personal achievements in life and the goodness we share with those around us. We can contribute with our children, who are the future, by being good parents and good role models for them.

As you heal your broken heart, remember that no one can make your contribution for you. You own your spirit, and you must never, ever give anyone the power to crush it. Protect and preserve it at all costs because the more you grow out of your despair, the stronger and better it will become. And all of the good efforts of your life will be multiplied a hundredfold.

Maintain Your Sense of Humor

Think for a moment about all of the things you are free from now that your partner is gone. What's more, think that your newly found freedoms are his or her losses.

Females no longer have to be his secretary or pay his bills, run his errands, make his doctor appointments, or fold his laundry. You don't have to wake up at 6 a.m. to make his coffee and pack his lunch. You don't have to take care of his dog, write out his child support checks, or fight with the IRS on his behalf. You don't have to watch his favorite TV shows that you dislike or sit bored out of your mind while he watches sports. You don't have to put up with him going out with "the boys".

Let's not forget cleaning up after his messes, cooking his dinner, doing the dishes, helping him with his car repairs, taking care of him when he's (being a whimp---I mean) sick, and supporting him when no one else will. You no longer need to wait up for him because he has to work late. There are no more complaints from the peanut gallery about you wearing a sweatshirt and pants to bed.

You can turn the thermostat up as high as you want. You can still have leftovers after you order a pizza. You can go shopping and not have to worry about reporting how much you spent. You are allowed to look AND touch now.

Males have a substantially shorter list. Men will be free from fixing more than one car, doing home improvements, watching her soap operas, and killing those pesky spiders. Some men will be free from the regular closet search for clothes she's bought but has never worn. You know the credit card bills and receipts are hidden somewhere.

You no longer have to put up with her hours of conversation on the phone with friends and family, while you are trying to watch the game. You no longer have to put up with her nagging for help with the household chores or the kids. You no longer have to visit the in-laws when you'd rather be doing something more enjoyable like getting a root canal. You now qualify for the 20 items or less lane at the grocery store. You can turn the thermostat down as low as you want. You are allowed to look AND touch now.

Whether male or female, you should count your blessings every day. You have a lot to be thankful for.

Recover Your Self-esteem

You don't have just a broken heart. Your heart and life were broken, your spirit was crushed and I'm willing to bet that for some of you, your self-esteem vaporized the minute your partner closed the door.

You must realize that on a scale of 1 to 40, you are a 40, your partner left you for a 2, which makes him or her a zero! Just because your partner left doesn't mean you don't have value. You are not the one that changed. He or she is. As far as I'm concerned, you are worth 10,000 times that of your partner. Don't you dare let anyone on earth devalue your heart! Who knows you better than you do? No one. Believe in yourself and everyone else will too.

Ask the Hard Questions

You will reach a point in the healing process where you are ready to face the painful truths about your failed relationship. Emotionally stronger now, you will find yourself asking hard questions about your readiness to let your partner go or to work toward taking him or her back, if that is an option for you. Being able to honestly answer these questions gives you the power to move on to a better life with or without your partner.

Does He or She Value Your Love?

It's human nature to believe that after your partner sees the alternatives aren't so great, he or she will have regrets and return to you. You may convince yourself that he or she will soon "see the light".

The sad truth is, your partner may never see leaving you as a mistake; and if they do, it could take them years.

He or she may or may not return, and you may or may not want him or her back. In any case, you must be prepared for what comes next and do what's right for you through it all.

At first, I refused to give up on my marriage because I believed, more than anything else, that our love was strong, deep and real, and worth fighting to save. I believed, for a time, that indeed there was a chance for us. But I was soon forced to accept my reality, which was that I was the only one believing in our love.

Your partner has to value your relationship as much as you do. Remember, if he had done so, he never would have left in the first place. The one you love must return your love; if he doesn't, admit to yourself that it's all over.

Would You Take Your Partner Back? Why? What Will it Cost You?

Due to the self-preservation instinct we all have, heartbreakers rarely look back. They know they will never be perfect in your eyes again. They give up without a fight, never realizing the struggle within them will rage on until they face it and confront it.

Those who do realize their mistake in judgment and who are truly, deeply remorseful and willing to explore the issues that made them want to walk away, should at least try to go back. Many of you can forgive and get past the tragedy. You should be given the chance to repair your relationship if you desire to do so.

In the event he or she does return, be prepared. The temptation to open the door may be overwhelming. Before you do, examine the reasons behind their reappearance. Has the girlfriend or boyfriend just tossed them out of the house? Have they experienced their own brand of betrayal first-hand by catching their partner with someone else? Did he or she spend too much money or demand too much?

Your partner may be thinking that they can come back to you just long enough to "regroup" because the only thing really concerning them is that they need a place to stay. Sad, isn't it? It's sad that some people will use their previous partner that way. But some do.

Whatever the reason, chances are your partner is back because he or she knows you are lonely and vulnerable, and that part of you still cares. You are safe, dependable, and trustworthy—characteristics they do not deserve, I might add. If any of the above scenarios apply to you, it's probably best not to unlock the door, never mind opening it.

One of the first things you must ask yourself is this: "Is there any love left to save"? If so, why do you want to save it? Are you ready to forgive? Are you ready to accept the fact that nothing will ever be the same, that the relationship must be different now? Will the changes you both have to make cost too much of yourselves?

It may help you to make a "pros and cons" list. After it is complete, determine how many benefits exist compared to the negatives that must be overcome if you get back together. Once you make the evaluation—and only *you* can do it—you may be surprised at how you feel about things.

In my case, reconciliation was not possible because, after all, it would have required too much effort on his part. If he saw the value in searching his heart for answers, he would have already done it.

Draw your own conclusions, as I did. Recognize that despite your vulnerabilities you must be strong-willed and clear-headed. Remember, this is *your* life we're talking about. Don't allow your previous partner to unravel everything you've accomplished in recovery. Let your head rule your heart for a while.

What If Your Partner Wants You Back After You Have Moved On?

If you've moved on, your partner has probably been out of your life for a while. You've had time to heal the wounds, and you've likely taken the journey of self-discovery and found that you're OK, if not better now. You know how to be happy by yourself, and you may be prepared to be with someone else again.

By this time, you may decide that it's better to leave your life the way it is, without him or her in it. You may find, after talking with your partner, that he or she really hasn't changed. Again, question the motives behind the return. Is he or she only returning because they feel familiar and comfortable with you? How do *you* feel?

Then again, he or she may be finding out for themselves that they made a terrible mistake and your partner may be genuinely remorseful for having broken your trust and your heart. Some people do realize their mistake in judgment. They can be truly, deeply remorseful and willing to explore the issues that made them want to walk away. To be given an honest and welcome chance to repair your relationship is a blessing few can hope for. If this is the desire of your heart and you both are ready to explore the pain, then you must also forgive and begin afresh.

If he or she comes back to you, you will find yourself at a critical crossroad in your life. Repair your relationship only if it is right for you. Give yourself all the time you need to make your decision wisely.

Are You Better Off Without Your Partner?

Before you decide whether to take him or her back, make sure you take a walk down nightmare lane—you know the road to hell you went down after he or she left. Remember every detail of how you were kicked to the curb like Tuesday's trash and how your partner never looked back. Remember how you told the love of your life that you wanted to die and all he or she could say was "I'm sorry". Remember the lies and the unreturned phone calls. Don't forget, too, that he or she sleeps with someone else now.

Ask yourself why you would take someone like this back. A lot of women and men would rather take their spouses back simply because it's easier than facing a life without them. If you do choose to take your partner back, don't be fooled. Unless they are willing to go through the intense effort of rebuilding the relationship properly, you must be prepared on some level to go through the heartache all over again, because he or she is returning with no guarantees. Five years down the road, you may be rereading this book.

Make all life-changing decisions involving love with the utmost of care. When figuring out what's best for you, look at all of the components present in solid, happy, and lasting relationships. Some of these are:

Lasting Love
Honor and Respect for Each Other
Compatibility
Physical Love
Friendship and Support of Each Other

Looking at these characteristics in their simplest form, you might agree that they are obtainable with practically anyone at anytime. Only with the right one, though, will they hold strong through the ups and downs of any healthy, meaningful relationship.

If you don't feel that these vital elements can be achieved and made to last with the one you love, then it's time to face it and find someone who *will* make it happen.

On the other hand, if both of you are willing to give it all you've got, go for it. Some relationships *can* be saved and many are because the two individuals involved really want it to work this time. Both agree to work on the causes of the breakup and, together, they mend the broken heart and the broken trust. Metaphorically speaking, they push the boulder up the mountain until it rests on the summit.

These couples get there only through hard work, a lot of soul searching, communicating, crying, compromising, and forgiving. In the process both reveal their fears, inadequacies, and soulful needs. Trust is slowly won again as each works to heal the other.

As a result, what is rebuilt is more solid even than before. Though the heartbreak has forever changed the relationship, with the sincere and unceasing effort of both partners, it can turn out to be a better one.

This kind of change is actually a metamorphosis of sorts, a complete changing of a tragedy into a victory. And it cannot happen overnight. It's a painful journey that two people take **together**.

Is such an effort worth it? I think so, as long as both of you truly want to stay together. If starting over is where your heart *and mind* take you, please read my chapter on Forgiveness.

Time For Your Reality Check

I still had a glimmer of hope for my marriage until the day I checked reality. Your reality check may not reveal anything new. Mine revealed volumes.

Being completely shell-shocked, I couldn't search for answers for some time after he left. But eventually, my need to know the reasons overpowered my grief, and I began a quest for details.

After you've had time to grieve, and you've regained some sort of normalcy in your daily routine, you may find yourself still searching for answers about what actually took place prior to your breakup.

I tried to make some sense of my husband's leaving—I had seen no clues prior to our breakup. Unfortunately, I wasn't aware that I should be looking for them. As it was, I had no idea what turns my life would soon be taking.

I believed and trusted my husband until the day he left, six days after his return home after taking a three-month, out-of-state school course. During this absence he seemed to be growing distant. I just assumed he was depressed because he was so far away from home. Then I noticed the unusually high phone bill and a multitude of calls to a strange number. I asked about these things and believed his "explanation". Only later, would I discover that he had been lying to me for months.

When I was ready, I did my own reality check. A Reality Check is the sobering act of discovering facts and accepting them despite what they reveal and how much it hurts. When I finally got up the courage to look for reasons, my discoveries crushed me to the very core. A cursory investigation led to a woman who worked at a convenience store near his job. Something must have gradually developed between them, intensifying just before his time away at school. I think he was flattered by her attention and tempted by the picture she painted of how she would treat him if they were together. After all, she could promise anything because she had nothing to lose but her self-respect.

They became obsessed with one another, and spoke every day while he was away, often many times a day. He called her the very minute I left him after a visit at his school, a discovery that stabbed me in the heart. The record showed only one day of no calls between them. I deducted that they didn't need to call each other if they were together that day. The last chip fell into place.

Though the day of my Reality Check was heartbreaking, in a way it was also empowering. In those moments of discovery, I knew I no longer wanted to be married to someone so cruel. Despite his insistence that he never cheated on me, I had to accept the fact that my beloved husband was a liar, and he didn't love me as I loved him.

On that day, I forced myself to acknowledge the fact that people do sometimes break their sacred vows. And my husband had broken his. I mentally questioned those who can cheat and then live with themselves afterward, even

trying to justify their actions. If they aren't happy with
the life they have, why don't they leave first and then find
someone else? How can they say, "I love you" when they
don't? You don't cheat on someone you love.

The only answer I could arrive at is that the leaving
isn't about us. The reason lies in what is missing in them.
You can't fix it or change it. Only *they* can do that.

The Reality Check is a heart-wrenching experience
but, in my opinion, a necessary one. Believe it or not, your
discovery of the truth will fuel your recovery. It will make
you more determined than ever to succeed. It will confirm
what you already knew but were afraid to say out loud—
you are better off without your partner.

Following are a few quotes about betrayal by Sylvia
Browne. They are found in her book, *A Psychic's Guide to
Our World and Beyond—The Other Side and Back*:

Overcoming betrayal by someone you loved and trusted
isn't so easy. I wish I could promise you that if you're smart
enough, or alert enough, or careful enough, or a good enough
person, you'll never be betrayed. As it is, I can only promise
you that you can, will and must survive it if it happens to

you—if only to keep your betrayer from getting the added satisfaction of destroying you.

Unfortunately, good people are the easiest to betray, for a perfectly logical reason. Because we see the world only through our own eyes, and we assume that everyone thinks just like we do, it doesn't occur to us to stay on constant alert for deceit and lies and back-stabbing, particularly from someone we love who claims to love us.

Recovery from betrayal is very much like recovery from a loved one's death. You go through denial, grief, anger, self-pity, and self-recrimination. They can't be avoided, but keep an important goal in mind—let yourself feel them for the purpose of getting them out of your system, not for obsessing over the betrayal to the point that you can't move on. There is life after betrayal, take it from me. Here are a few tips, some of which I learned the hard way:

The answer to "How could I have been so gullible/ stupid / blind"? is, "by believing that everyone's mind and heart work like yours". They don't. It's that simple. There are other good people like you out there, and the sooner you pick yourself up and walk away, the sooner you'll find them.

The answer to "how could they do this to me if they loved me"? is, "Their spirit has a longer way to go on its journey than yours does, or they wouldn't put so little value on love". It's their lesson to learn, which they may or may not accomplish in this lifetime.

It's not your job to teach them whether they want to learn it or not. They won't learn until they're ready, any more than a kindergarten student is ready to learn nuclear physics.

Take a long, honest look not at who you wanted him to be but at who the evidence proves he really is; recognize that his spiritual limits, not yours, caused the betrayal to happen—and let it go.

The adage "Actions speak louder than words" has become such a cliché that we forget how important it is. When there's a contradiction between what someone says and what he does, ignore the words—the truth is in the behavior every time. Hearing "I love you" from someone who's plunging a knife between your shoulder blades does not mean, "Love is a knife between the shoulder blades". It means, "This person is deliberately hurting me, and that's not love"!

5

Forgiveness

The Inner Struggle

How can you be so disappointed in someone and still love them? The struggle inside you is about loving versus letting go. You know that letting go is for your own good, but something inside still wants to hang on.

I think what we cling to are all the good memories—the love and security we once felt and never wanted to lose. Clinging to what is lost, though, causes nothing but pain. Think of how you feel every time you mention the name of the one you loved and lost.

Can we do both? Can we let go of the pain *and* forgive so that we can continue to love? The heart wants what the heart wants and we have to remember that our brains are not engaged when it comes to the heart.

Can we really blame men and women for being idiots for leaving? After all, a lot of the time men are thinking with the wrong equipment! They're not thinking with the head that holds their brain. No they are thinking with their little head if you know what I mean. I think some of the women aren't thinking at all. There's something you have to keep remembering. This is not your loss. It is your partner's loss. When you are able to say these words, you have gained the strength and desire to forgive and move on. When you do, you will revel at the fact that you were able to rise from the ashes of the broken trust and betrayal. We also have to remember: the RIGHT one never leaves. If the WRONG one has left you in the dust, this simply means that the RIGHT one will be along soon enough.

Is There Forgiveness?

Forgiving your betrayer is a choice you must eventually make, whether or not you have the chance to offer forgiveness to their face. When you take advantage of an opportunity to forgive, you help free yourself from the pain.

At first, I thought forgiveness had to be earned, but the truth is, if you don't forgive, you really can't move on. There will always be that little piece of you dragging around a freight load of luggage packed with bitterness. For me, forgiveness is all about giving myself the ability to let go and move on. Forgiveness is not a gift to your betrayer. Forgiveness is a gift to yourself. You deserve this gift.

I feel sorry for those who have something wonderful and don't recognize it for what it is. I am saddened because they can walk away without a second glance back. They don't see themselves as the loser right now, but I'm willing to bet in time they will.

Moving on is all about having yet another chance to start a new life. It's a gift, actually—another chance to start over and get it right. You are older and much wiser and you can rebuild it any way you want. For a change, you don't have to be concerned with the opinions or desires of anyone else.

Build your new life and then find someone who fits into it. Find someone who will love it just as you do. The right person will share in it and contribute to make it even better. This person will be your best friend and your partner, not someone just along for the ride.

Living without forgiving keeps you locked in a past that holds no future for you. Time moves on while you stand still. While you're standing still, opportunities for future happiness are passing you by. You can't grab on to those opportunities in the future while still holding on to the past. The past is done. Nothing can change it. Let it go.

Life is full of choices. You can stay locked in the past or you can jump on that roller coaster called life and trust in yourself to be happy and alive. It's your choice.

Unpacking Your Emotional Baggage

Breaking up is hard to do but moving on afterwards is even harder. Learning how to unpack your emotional baggage is one of the most important steps toward letting go and closing the door for good.

Breakup baggage is much like the baggage you take on a long trip to a place you have never been. You're not quite sure what to pack so you wind up packing a little of everything. You realize when you finally reach your destination that you have packed many things you don't need at all.

The desired destination in this case is your readiness to move on with your life. You may feel ready but you cannot truly let go of your pain without first unpacking the emotional baggage associated with it.

Metaphorically speaking, unpack every issue in those bags and lay them out for your inspection. Examine each closely, one by one. Now is the time to decide why you packed these issues to begin with, and why they now need to be discarded.

Some Things You May Have Packed By Mistake

- ***Tapes:*** The negative tapes that keep playing over and over in your head.
  Tape 1 I know we will get back together.
  Tape 2 I am not worthy of being loved.
  Tape 3 If I love again, I will be hurt again.
- **Mementos from the Broken Relationship**
- ***Mutual Friends***

Why You Packed These Issues

The tapes you packed are all created by you in an attempt to help you make sense of the breakup.

The mementos are familiar and allow you to hold on to the good memories you have of the relationship. They serve as proof somehow that your love was real.

Mutual friends sometimes serve as a lifeline to your ex, which you are not yet ready to release.

Why You Need to Resolve the Issues, Then Throw Them Out

Most of the tapes created during and after a breakup are negative and quite damaging. If you continue to play them, you will soon believe them. Most of the time, the reality of your situation is completely opposite of what your tapes say. It is natural to hope to be reunited with someone you love but it is very important to admit what the real chances are of that happening. You must stop yourself from believing you are not worthy of being loved. You absolutely are! The important thing with this tape is it will continue to play until you learn to love yourself again and realize that every person offers a tremendous value to the world—especially you! If others choose not to see that, it is their loss. If you are afraid to love again because you may be hurt, you must remember that finding real and lasting love IS worth kissing a few frogs along the way. You just need to be a little more proficient at detecting them.

Hanging on to sweet mementos of your relationship only perpetuates your need to hang on to the past. Discard all reminders so that you can move on.

Mutual friends are okay to keep as long as you do not use them as a lifeline to keep tabs on your ex's life. If you and your friends respect each other, you will limit the topics of conversation to anything but your ex.

When to Unpack

The process of unpacking your emotional baggage typically begins around six months after the breakup. This is because, it usually takes about six months before you begin to feel more like yourself and regain your self-esteem and confidence. The actual unpacking can then begin and take anywhere from six months to a year. It is very important that you perform this grueling act of self-introspection BEFORE you start dating again. If you do try to date before you are ready, the experience could wind up as a train wreck. I know of one woman who went to a club a few months after a breakup and spent part of the time in the bathroom crying. She was crying because the DJ played the Toni Braxton hit, "Unbreak My Heart". Her date felt helpless.

Your perspective partner doesn't deserve having to sift through the wreckage of your recent trauma. Before involving someone else in your life, you must be present in your own and ready to move forward.

The last thing anyone wants to do is hold a place open for the ex.

When to Stop Unpacking

Although dealing with emotional baggage can be an ongoing event, the majority of the unpacking can stop when the following things are true:

1. You can smile again and appreciate everything life has to offer….good and bad.
2. You remember why you liked the song that used to make you cry.
3. You can say that you are truly happy with yourself and your life.

4. You know who you are and what you want out of life and you have made plans to move forward to make it happen.
5. You look forward to sharing your love and trust with someone else because you know you can, without hesitation or reservation.

Keep in mind however that sometimes, little items you thought were unpacked and gone tend to resurface when you least expect them. Be ready to put them back in their place where they belong....out of your life and heart.

Letting Go and Closing the Door

After you've checked reality, unpacked your emotional baggage and when you are ready, you must close the door and walk away. You must accept this challenge in your life for something you can't change. You must learn to overcome the pain, move away from the past and live in this moment.

Letting go of the greatest love I've ever known was the hardest thing I've ever done in my life. But I did it, and so can you. You must advance your recovery however possible.

Picking Up The Pieces

After my personal Reality Check, I made a list of all the hurtful things my husband had said or done over the last few months. Looking at the cold words on paper, I determined that the man my husband had become didn't deserve someone like me. And I certainly didn't deserve to be treated the way I was when he left.

Find a way to give yourself "closure" even if your partner won't. I wrote my husband a letter of good-bye. I wrote to him about all of the things that had gone unsaid. Things that I felt he needed to know about how I felt about him, his betrayal, the pending divorce and my forgiveness of those things. When I put the envelope in the mailbox, I finally had my closure.

You too, may find comfort in performing some kind of similar ritual. Validate the positive things, which have come from this emotional storm and know that God never closes a door without opening a window. Your future lies ahead. Embrace this wonderful future and have faith in it and yourself.

6

Rebuilding Your New Life

Examining Your Life Events

I believe everything, good or bad, happens for reasons we don't understand, mainly because life goes by in a blur. If you stop long enough to look at significant events in your life, you will probably be able to make some sense of them. For no other reason than to take an assessment of your life thus far, I encourage you to analyze your part (as well as the part of other major players) in each significant life event you've had. For each event, ask yourself the following questions:

What good came out of this event?
What bad came out of this event?
What lesson did I learn?

What lesson did you teach someone else?
Why do you think this event happened?
What did this event lead you to do next?

Write down all of the significant life events you've had and see if you notice a pattern. I think when you are done taking account of your life, you will be astonished at the doors you are able to open for yourself and proud of the doors you are finally able to close.

A Significant Life Event

For me, "playing fair" has been a lifelong goal—and lifelong mistake. My sense of fair play has always seemed to be out of proportion with everyone else's. I wind up getting hurt because I play fair when no one else does.

My mother loves to tell the story about when I was four or five years old. At the time, a little boy persistently bullied me. He pulled and pulled my hair until I would cry.

After my mother found out, she gave me a baton and told me to whack him with it the next time he pulled my hair.

Well, he did it again, and I went crying to my mother. She asked me if I hit him with the baton, and I said, "no". When she asked why not, I answered, "Because he wouldn't turn around"!

The truth is, no one is waiting for you to turn around. We live in a world where everyone makes his or her own rules, and no one else has the rulebook.

Take it from me, I learned the hard way that you must take back what is yours, whatever that might be—namely, your heart, your life, your self-esteem. If you're being ignored, do it right back. If someone has something of yours, reclaim it. Stand up for yourself.

Finding the Patterns in Past Mistakes

Over the years, I have realized the need to periodically make adjustments to my attitude about myself, and to make adjustments to my life that will keep me from making the same mistakes.

Many people believe in fate and, in doing so, are able to accept life's bumps in the road much easier than the rest of us. However, I find myself wondering about "the grand plan" and what it has in store for me.

When I look back over my life and all of the bad things that have happened, I can see sort of a pattern. Many of the bad things that have happened to me have opened up doors and pathways to some wonderful experiences and valuable lessons I now believe I needed to learn.

Take, for example, my father's stroke. At the time of this serious event, I was the only one of my siblings acting as caretaker for my dad. I was separated from my first husband, and had just started a new job. To say the least, I was on emotional overload. But the result was that all this anxiety led me to seek God for comfort and guidance. I found a religion and for the first time in my life, I began to feel at peace.

Likewise, if you have ever wondered why we as human beings find achieving complete happiness in life and relationships such a struggle, then you should devote the time to yourself and your spirit within to find out why. The answer is uniquely different for each one of us. You owe it to yourself and the ones you love to find out why your life takes unexpected turns down roads you wouldn't normally plan to travel. The roads you have been down in the past leave a trail of lessons and tell a story, begging not to be heard, but understood.

Gaining the understanding of the past mistakes you have made in life and love doesn't guarantee a life without future mistakes or regrets, but it does arm you with the knowledge of what did not work for you in the past. Knowing where and why you failed yourself in the past allows you to commit to moving forward on the journey of life and love, ever aware of possible potholes in the winding road.

Learning from our mistakes lends a flavor of acceptance for why things have happened in the past and allows us the long awaited ability to finally add closure to issues that have haunted us for years. Better still, this newly found self-taught education on life and love prepares us to be better human beings for whatever may come next.

In order to learn from your mistakes in love or life, you must first identify the patterns of behavior in your current and past relationships. Then determine which of those behaviors are destructive to a healthy relationship. Next, you must uncover the lesson to be learned and decide what you will do differently in the future. Finally, make this

proposed behavior change a steadfast, non-negotiable rule
for future relationships.

Here is an example to use as a guide.

List Your Dating Patterns of Behavior:

- Past and present partners have been younger
- Past and present partners earn less money
- Past and present partners are less educated
- Past and present partners have had dissimilar interests
- Most partners are difficult to communicate with

Lesson Learned:

In this example, common sense should tell you that
if you are always dating partners with whom you have a
difficult time communicating due to age or education, then
you should date older, more educated partners in the future.
If you find that earning more money than your partner
is a problem which may result in jealousy or feelings of
inadequacy, then you should set the bar higher next time
and date partners who are equally stable financially.

In theory, these love lesson principles sound simple and
easy, and they are, if applied to your real life. The hard part

is teaching yourself to become increasingly aware that there is a lesson in just about everything we do. There is also a ripple effect from our actions that extends not only to us, but everyone with whom we interact. From this moment on, make a commitment to yourself to be alert to the lessons that life and love are teaching you. Pay attention to the signs along the way for the sake of your happiness and spiritual wellbeing. You will soon find, when your journey of life and love leads to a crossroad, you will be better prepared emotionally to decide the best path for you.

Everything we do makes us what we are today. Every person we help or hurt, every contribution to society and family, affects the world in some small way. Every person on earth is here for a reason. Every experience we have is a lesson. Pay attention and learn.

My Relationships
and The Lessons Learned

My first important relationship was with my first husband. We were together for 12 years. I thought I knew what love was when I married him. It felt like love. After all, we were pretty compatible in most areas. We rarely fought and were faithful to each other.

We had a lot to learn. In truth, very little meaningful communication passed between us. The first five years were pretty good, but I was young and naïve and had no benchmark against which to measure true love. Gradually, we began to just go through the motions, and tolerance took the place of love.

Although he is a good man with good intentions, I slowly realized he had a serious drinking problem. This was compounded when he was diagnosed with manic depression five years into the marriage. I won't go into the details, but trust me when I say, I learned from this experience that you can't "fix" someone else. People with problems like these will only attempt to fix them if they see a benefit in it for them. Unfortunately, the feelings of others rarely come in to play when it comes to their motivation.

After the separation and divorce, it took three years before I even had the desire to venture out into the dating world again. A year later, I thought I had found love again. But I couldn't have been more wrong. My next relationship was with the person I now call "Satan from Hell". At first this man was charming and loving. He made me laugh, and God knows, I needed some laughter.

Unfortunately, I was still naive and trusting. Before I knew it, this person had me supporting him financially. This was in addition to supporting my young son and myself. He too was an alcoholic and abusive as well. As if that weren't bad enough, I later found that he was stealing money from me for a drug habit I never knew he had. I very nearly had to file for bankruptcy, but I got rid of him instead.

It took me a long time to figure out how to do it because he refused to leave. I knew that if I just put him out and changed the locks, he would still find a way to either seriously harm me or make my life even more miserable.

Finally, I put my house up for rent and moved in with my mother temporarily. This action forced him to leave the state. As soon as he was gone, I moved back to my own home and endured a long journey of financial recovery.

The lessons I learned from this were how to survive financially and to never allow another person into my life who doesn't truly love and respect me.

Two years later, after that relationship ended, I gave up looking. I no longer believed my white knight in shining armor still existed. Then I met him—the one who took my breath away.

You know the saying: "You don't miss what you never had"? Until I met my second husband, I had no idea love like this was possible. The love I had felt for those before him was nothing compared to the love I felt for him. He was simply the love of my life.

This kind of love overwhelmed me and filled me up with complete joy. It carried me to heights of happiness I had never known before. For two great years, I was allowed to experience this kind of love.

That all changed abruptly the day my husband woke up and decided he didn't love me enough to stay faithful. The cruelest part of the betrayal was that he remained as loving to me as he always had been—up until a few days before he left. I had no idea anything was wrong until then, but by that time, he had already made up his mind and planned his departure to his next victim.

I still maintain that if he couldn't be happy with the kind of love we shared then he will never last with anyone else.

What I Learned

I learned many valuable lessons from my experience with despair. I learned that life is too short to spend it working all the time. To those workaholics like myself, you may miss important signals from the one you love—signals that you can't afford to miss.

I learned that even though you may bet your life on how well you know someone and what they are capable of, you can lose that bet.

I learned to make time for myself.

I learned that some people are never satisfied, and that love means nothing unless it is returned.

I learned that the deep sorrow I felt over the breakup of my marriage caused me to gain knowledge and to grow emotionally. My experience, knowledge and growth can help others.

I learned that I should be more cautious and spend more time finding out about the person I care for before allowing my heart to take over my head.

I learned that I can never again afford to make someone else my whole life, because one day, he may walk out the door with it.

I learned to never give up on myself.

I learned that happiness is something we achieve. That it is not a gift we receive from someone else.

I learned that if I could survive losing the love of my life, the rest of my life should be a piece of cake.

I learned that it's important to develop your own life, independent from anyone else you may love. The life you develop will be your retreat when you need it.

Looking Hopefully Down the Road

It gives me a lot of peace to feel I've made a little sense of the crazy twists and turns that my life has taken.

I would also like to think the lives of those I've loved have been enriched in some way by having me in their life, even for a short time.

I believe our destination in life is predetermined before we're born. The journey we take to arrive there is up to us. Whatever paths we take, right or wrong, I don't believe we travel the journey alone.

When I look down the road to what may lie ahead, I feel hopeful. Hopeful that it will finally be my turn to be happy, long term, with someone I can love, someone who will love me just as much in return.

I find myself thinking of life as a series of optional paths we can take along the journey. Think of three paths you can take right now in your current situation. Think what could happen on the way along each path. Ask yourself if each path will bring you closer to your destination, or if it will cause you to backtrack or go in circles.

Do some paths have obstacles where some don't? Is it better to face the obstacles than to just choose an easier path? Focus on the direction in which you should be heading. Choose your path wisely because undoubtedly, another adventure awaits you with another lesson to learn.

Pure-Hearts, Dark-Hearts, and Half-Hearts

By examining *my* life events, I was able to put a lot of things into perspective. I learned that there seem to be three basic kinds of people in our world: Pure-Hearts, Dark-Hearts and Half-Hearts. Studying these personalities helped me to realize the types of people I want to avoid and the types with which I want to surround myself.

Pure-Hearts

Pure-Hearts are those people who are optimistic, happy, and naïve. They always see the good in people, and they go through life thinking most people are like them. Pure-Hearts never have ulterior motives for good deeds and are shocked at people who do.

Pure-Hearts never expect bad things to happen to them because they know they don't deserve it. Yet, when bad things do befall them, they take it in stride and try to learn and grow from the experience. Pure-Hearts love and give without expecting anything in return. Pure-Hearts are a joy to be around.

Dark-Hearts

Dark-Hearts are those people who wake up with no other agenda than destroying the lives of others for their own betterment. Dark-Hearts have no conscience or morals. They go through life believing the world owes them something for being alive, and every day they set out to collect on the debt. These people are a plague on humanity.

Half-Hearts

Half-Hearts are those people who, for one reason or another, live their lives as part-time Pure-Heart and part-time Dark-Heart. If they really try, these people can be great most of the time. But it's the Dark-Heart in them that keeps them from succeeding in life and being truly happy.

Half-Hearts have unresolved dark issues. They want to be completely pure but they don't know how to rid themselves of the dark side. These people need deep introspection to conquer the demons within. Unfortunately, most don't know what those demons are, and if they do, they don't consider them important enough to go through the pain of facing and exorcising them. Half-Hearts live half-lives.

Half-Hearts have no problem leaving a loving relationship. The person they once loved hasn't changed, but they have somehow, and they have no idea why the change occurred or even how to fix it.

Somewhere along the line, Half-Hearts have been demoralized and criticized or raised to believe their life has very little value and will never amount to much. They are very insecure, even when those around them show them love and support. Many are confused about what is morally right and wrong. Some wind up abusing drugs and alcohol to self-medicate the ever-present anxiety they feel.

After reaching conclusions about what kinds of people breathe the same air I do, I realized that most of the time, I have had relationships with Half-Hearts. I knew that they had issues I couldn't fix for them. They are great people, but they will suck the life right out of you if you let them. I don't know about you, but I've paid my dues trying to love this kind of person.

Half-Hearts don't know how to love back in the same way Pure-Hearts do. Therefore, I have resolved to avoid anyone but a Pure-Heart. This is the only type of person I really understand.

Deciding What You Want Out of Your New Life

Your pain may still be deep right now because you made your ex the only focus of your life. You allowed yourself to be defined by him or her. I know, because I did the same thing. Like so many other women, I thought that kind of complete devotion was all part of being a good wife. When a man leaves a woman who thinks this way, he takes her life with him.

The time has come to create a new life, one that will never be subject to walking out the door. It's a hard lesson to learn and an even harder task to pull off, but you must learn it. Learn to share your love without losing your identity or your own soulful purpose in life. Be independent. Learn to be happy alone. I'm willing to bet you won't be alone for long.

Sculpt Your New Future

Think of your new life as a ball of clay. You, as the sculptor, have an idea of what this ball of clay should look like when you're finished molding and sculpting. You begin to mold it to resemble that idea. Keep in mind, you may make mistakes along the way, but you have the power to remold and fix them. You have the power of perfection. You can mold your clay into anything. Think big. Set great and wonderful goals, and don't stop sculpting your clay until you are completely happy with the results.

Think of all of the elements present in life: your attitude, your looks, your finances, your home, your relationship with your children, your family, your job, your hobbies, your love life and your goals. What needs work and what doesn't? If you had to pick one thing to work on first, what would it be? Once you know what it is, draw a mental map of how you are going to get there and what you are going to have to do to reach your destination.

Reaching Short-Term and Long-Term Goals

Decide on meaningful goals that you want to achieve, whether large or small in scale. My goals included completing small and large home repairs, then everything from designing and creating my own sleepwear to upholstering my furniture. I decided to landscape my yard, plan parties, travel to Hawaii, and go to Disney World. I was determined to write my book and create my web site. Finally, I set goals to lose weight and to rediscover my lost spirit.

I wrote down every one of these goals and listed the steps needed to achieve them. By actually writing my goals down, I made a commitment to accomplishing them. Also, I could better organize things on paper. Once they were written, I found I had many short-term goals that would be fairly easy to reach.

I also had a lot of long-term goals that would take a fair amount of time and money to achieve. In order to meet my more ambitious goals, I prioritized the steps needed to achieve them. Then I worked those steps into my daily life a little at a time. I identified obstacles that might prevent me from completing certain goals and decided how to eliminate those obstacles—or at least go around them.

I have to tell you, there were times when I felt I had bitten off more that I could chew. But I refused to give up. To give up, would be like breaking a promise to myself, and I had had enough broken promises in my life. You know what? I was tired of it.

Achieving your goals and feeling yourself smile and beam from within is a gift you give yourself. It feels great and warm and wonderful. It makes you feel alive. When you are accomplishing positive things for yourself, you wake up every day eager to achieve more.

After only a year of determined goal setting, I found I had achieved more than half my goals. I feel great pride in myself for having the ability to see them through to the end and for remaining committed to accomplishing the rest.

You may be wondering how I could do all of this while nursing my broken heart. The truth is, it wasn't easy. I thought of my husband a million times a day. So, a million times a day I consciously pushed him out of my head to focus on something much more important. He had received the best part of me already, and I wasn't about to let him take the rest. If your heart still hurts, you must think the same in setting and reaching your goals.

It doesn't matter *where* you start, only that you *do* start. Again, I encourage you to think big. The only thing standing in your way is you, so get out of your own way. Have fun and good luck!

7

Relationships and Revelations

Why do some relationships work and others fail? In answering this question, I have tried to analyze the relationships of a few couples I know.

Katrina and Jeff

Katrina and Jeff met as co-workers. They became great friends because they had a lot in common. Each was getting over a hellish relationship. Because they were friends first, they were each given the rare opportunity to see the vulnerable side of the other. They witnessed each other's strength to overcome grief and move on.

Katrina and Jeff leaned on each other through it all and emerged as partners. Already best friends, they couldn't help eventually falling in love. As an observer, I thought it strange at first that there were few public displays of affection between them. After getting to know them though, I saw that they are playful and happy, and have a mutual respect for each other. Katrina and Jeff can count on each other, no matter what. This relationship will last.

Jolene and Andy

Another couple I know, Jolene and Andy, had been married more than 35 years when Andy decided that he wanted to live apart. Jolene was devastated. You may be thinking what the point is in parting after so many years together. Unfortunately, a split after a long marriage is actually becoming more commonplace.

Andy still loves Jolene very much, but as a best friend only. They still have occasional dinners together and see each other often. Andy seems to have wanted more or maybe less of something. I'm not really sure. The two have a lot in common, but they also have very different personalities. Jolene loves to go out, and Andy is more of a solitary soul.

This relationship didn't last, but it evolved into one of friendship. In any event, Jolene wants Andy to be happy even if it breaks her heart to let go.

Barbara and David

Barbara and David lived together for a couple of years and then split when David was caught cheating. After a year of dating other people, they got back together. Barbara is a very pretty girl with a great personality. She could have anyone she wants.

I asked Barbara why she took David back. She explained that, for one thing, he showed her in many different ways how sorry he was for hurting her and she believes he will not stray again. But she is also a realist. While believing that everyone deserves a second chance, she says if it does happen again, it won't hurt as much as it did the first time.

Barbara has a shield surrounding her heart that protects her, but also prevents her from truly trusting and loving with all that she has. Barbara and David have a comfortable and easygoing life together. Neither places any demands on the other. Each is free to pursue what ever makes him or her happy.

Will this relationship last? So far, it has. But I can't help feeling that there is a lot of emptiness here.

Me and My Husband

To all who knew the two of us, we were the perfect couple. Rarely seen apart, we were always holding hands, hugging each other and kissing any time we felt like it, which was often. We were happy and loving to each other, and had built a life together on some wonderful memories as newlyweds. We enjoyed exploring life together and seeing the world through each other's eyes. We had hopes and dreams that we wanted to achieve together.

For the first time in my life, I was truly happy. I entrusted him completely with my naked, naïve, and vulnerable soul to hold in his heart. I loved him totally and completely. From my perspective, our love and marriage were perfect and unbreakable. He told me he had never been happier in his life, and I believe that was and is still true.

For months after he left, I was determined to not give up on him. I felt that a love like ours was worth fighting for. At first I thought the connection between us was so deep that, sooner or later, he would realize what he had walked away from. But the more time that went by without any contact from him, the more I came to realize just how one-sided our love really had been.

This relationship came to an end because my husband wanted more—more love and more attention than any woman is capable of giving without totally losing herself in the process. I completely devoted myself to him and yet that still was not enough.

There were things he couldn't share with me, things he kept hidden deep within himself. He seemed to be unable to control his secret desires. He harbors dark thoughts for other people. And I believe he has intense feelings of insecurity and inferiority that he can't explain because he doesn't understand them himself.

I slowly also learned that he has an obsessive desire to achieve in life, no matter who he steps on in the process. He is in a constant state of change, moving from one job to another, and one woman to another, in the hopes that he will find perfection. Nothing and no one is ever good enough for very long. At least that has been the pattern.

Ultimately, I realized that I'd rather be alone the rest of my life than be with someone so deceptive and incapable of knowing the difference between once-in-a-lifetime love and run-of-the-mill infatuation.

8

Elements of a Lasting Relationship

What is the answer to the lifelong question, "What makes a relationship last"? Obviously, every relationship is complex, sometimes maddeningly so. We all want to be happy, but most of us aren't really sure if we are. If we are, we may not be sure if our partner is happy. Many of us may believe we're on the right track when, in reality, our partner walks with us—but down a separate road.

Before you begin a new relationship, you might find it helpful to study a few basic but vital truths that are consistent in lasting relationships.

Couples as Individuals

Couple is defined as follows: to connect for
consideration together. A man and a woman married,
engaged or otherwise paired. Two equal and opposite forces
that act along parallel lines.

Relationships that last have a lot going for them, as this
chapter reveals, but one vital element is that its partners
are traveling the same path, or moving along parallel lines,
as the definition above states. Partners can have the same
goals *and* remain individuals in their own right. These
couples are happy and secure because they allow each
other's individuality to remain intact while they make a
life's journey together. This is the way it should be.

Truth, Trust and Friendship

Truth is defined as follows: The body of real things,
events and facts. Actuality, fidelity, constancy, honesty.

All of us are guilty of telling little white lies to spare the feelings of others. For me, this is the only kind of acceptable lie. Any other kind of lie is destructive, pure and simple. Lies never stay hidden. The truth about them always seems to worm their way to the surface when the liar least wants it to.

Why then, do some people tell lies in their intimate relationships? Why do they feel that it's all right to leave something out of a conversation when doing so is basically the same thing as lying?

The answer is simple. They usually do it because a lie or an omission of the truth is prettier than the plain truth. The real truth strips people naked, in a sense, and renders them vulnerable to your acceptance or rejection.

I was raised to tell the truth, no matter what, because when a lie is uncovered, it only makes matters worse. When I tell the cold hard truth about something I know may compromise me in some way, I stand tall and ready for what may come. Your partner can't eat you for lunch, so tell the truth! What's the worst that can happen? Whatever the consequences of telling the truth, they are far better than living with the guilt of a lie. At the very least, the one you love deserves the truth. We all do. You should always expect the truth from the one you love and also provide the truth to the one you love. No matter what happens.

If you know that the truth about something will end up hurting the one you love, you must trust in the fact that getting over the painful truth is much easier than getting over the lie. I know this from experience. When you lie, you betray a trust, and trust is very hard to rebuild once it's gone.

Trust is defined as follows: Assured reliance on the character, ability, strength, or truth of someone or something. A change or duty imposed in faith or confidence or as a condition of some relationship.

Trust walks hand-in-hand with love. If you can trust him, you can love him—not the other way around. Trust is like someone handing you the key to heaven. Once you have it, you never want it to be taken away. Trust, like love, is all about being able to depend on your mate for anything or everything, at any time.

Though it is a coveted element in any relationship, trust is something that can be easily taken for granted and often is. It is also sometimes too soon and too freely given. You must be a careful judge of when and when *not* to trust someone completely.

Trusting Enough to Be Vulnerable

To trust is to allow your vulnerabilities to show. The only way to truly get to know someone intimately is to knock down walls and barriers that have been built up, often because of a previous breakup. Earning complete trust can be messy, as it involves kicking around emotional baggage and debris. But the rewards are truly worth the trouble.

Each time you reveal something about yourself to your partner, a layer of the wall between you is peeled away. The closer you get to removing the wall once and for all, the closer you will be to holding your partner's heart and soul in your hand. The ability to achieve this level of trust in each other is indeed heaven on earth.

Heartfelt revelations are precious and must not be taken lightly. We are, in these vulnerable situations, helpless as

97

babes. We are at the other's mercy as to how we will be treated from here on out.

Will your potential partner use this most private knowledge against you or will they use it to better understand and love you? How will you use his or her personal revelations?

You will survive the broken trust and betrayal in your relationship and be stronger for it. However, you will not be without battle scars. You will probably have to work very hard to trust again. You may have built a very high wall around yourself but once someone new earns your trust, it will have been worth all of the work.

You will have to go on your gut instincts here. Before you reveal too much of yourself, you must decide whether or not this person is worthy of your trust. Be patient as you explore the possibilities of any new potential partner. If it is meant to be, he or she will be patient as well.

Friendship is defined as follows: One attached to another by affection or esteem.

Your partner or mate should be your biggest fan, always in your corner even if they may think you're wrong. Do you know why? It's because they expect this from you in return. Friendship is a genuine mutual affection between two people. If your mate is also your best friend, then he or she will always be happy to be with you and will really care about you. To say that there is love in friendship is not far off the mark.

Friendship is one of many kinds of love. Friends tell each other things they would never dream of telling mere acquaintances or co-workers. Friends count on each other for advice and the voice of reason when their lives are spinning out of control.

Friends provide a safe harbor for us when we need space and perspective. The kind of person you are looking to fall in love with should provide this kind of friendship to you.

Commonality, Compromise, and Communication

I define *commonality* as follows: To have things, feelings, ideals, or goals in common.

Compromise is defined as follows: To come to agreement by mutual concession.

Commonality and compromise are two additional elements needed to sustain a lasting relationship. No one enjoys compromising, but we must accept that it is an inevitable part of any healthy relationship. The reason for our attraction to other people is not because they are mirror images of us. It is because they are different from us in many ways. Occasional compromising is the natural result of two separate personalities getting together.

Any two individuals will experience new things together and learn to see things from a different point of view. Getting to know someone different than us is an exciting adventure filled with surprises. This is all fine for friendships and short-term relationships, but for a bond to last, threads of commonality must exist upon which to build something meaningful.

These threads of commonality are the things not up for compromise. If you find you must compromise on issues that should be common between you, you're back to square one, involved in a one-sided relationship.

Only *you* can decide what you must have in common with a potential mate and what things you are willing to compromise without feeling taken advantage of. The good news is that it's pretty easy to find out where a new friend stands on these basic and vital issues, because you both should be asking a million questions about each other. If you don't like the answers, walk away. If you do like the answers, well you know what to do.

Communication is defined as follows: an exchange of information.

Just because you've gotten to the point of being able to finish each other's sentences doesn't mean you know every thought your mate has. You really only know the familiar ones. It is extremely important to voice your thoughts out loud so that they can be recognized and registered by the one you love. And it is just as important to encourage your mate to do the same. Never assume your partner will, or should, know how you feel. This would be a highly unlikely and unrealistic assumption. You can't read his or her mind either—although, I'm sure you wish you could.

Many couples fall into the trap of less and less communication. This trend is frequently interpreted as "being comfortable" with each other, which couldn't be further from the truth. In reality, for these people, a lack of communication simply means that they are too tired, unwilling or afraid to voice thoughts or opinions that will meet with opposition. These people are merely "settling". Deep down, they may eventually feel a slow burning resentment for not having a voice in their relationship.

For a relationship to be of lasting value, each partner must learn not only to *really listen* to the other, but also to determine what parts of communication are important and need further attention. Likewise, both partners need to feel that they are being *heard* and actually understood. A partner should try to learn why you said what you did and what these things really mean to you.

If you encounter problems that your partner can help with, by all means ask for help and resolve them together. After all, you are a couple—a team. Communicate like one.

No one wants to feel that they are just taking up space in someone else's world. Each of us wants to feel as though we are important in our partner's life. This feeling of belonging is the foundation for truth, trust and friendship, and the beginning of a beautiful, lasting relationship.

One Regret

If I had just one thing to do over again in my marriage, it would be to give my husband 30 minutes a day of uninterrupted conversation. I would have asked him about how his day went, explore any concerns he had, and talk about any new and exciting goals or dreams he'd been thinking about. I would have sat on his lap and looked deep into his beautiful brown eyes and told him just how very much I loved him.

In retrospect, I think he may have been able to communicate with me more than he actually did if we had just taken the time. We both got caught up in the humdrum of daily life. I don't know about him, but I have learned this lesson and don't intend to repeat this mistake.

Recognizing Unconditional Love

What is unconditional love and how can you tell when you have it? Love is an intangible emotion, which cannot be touched or seen. It can however, be witnessed by anyone with an open and willing heart. As the saying goes though, love is blind and telling the difference between mere infatuation and real love may be a difficult task at times.

Love comes in many forms

Infatuation has been defined as: Foolish and usually extravagant passion or love or admiration; Temporary love of an adolescent; and An object of extravagant short-lived passion.

Conditional love, or loving "if", is based on someone acting a certain way. In other words, someone who loves with conditions will love a person only if he or she behaves a certain way or lives his or her life in a manner pleasing to the other person.

Reasonable, logical love, or loving "because", is based on someone loving another because he or she has a certain characteristic or fulfills a need of the other person.

Unconditional love, or loving "in spite of", is based on someone loving another in spite of what has come to pass or what may come in the future. It is love with no strings attached. It is love without restriction, reservations or conditions. It is the desire to maintain pure love in spite of all odds or circumstances. Unconditional love is the one that will last a lifetime. This is the type of love everyone seeks. I know only one way to love, and I believe it's the right way—that is, all the way, with everything I've got. The romantic in me believes that getting hurt is worth the risk if, ultimately, it leads you to find that one pure love you can rely on. Pure love is worth just about anything.

It's the kind of love you wait a lifetime for, the kind that takes your breath away and makes you weak in the knees. It gives you wonderful butterflies in your stomach when you're about to see your love again. It's the kind of love that doesn't diminish over time but instead, grows stronger as time goes by.

Some people are in love with the notion of "being in love". After all, no one enjoys the thought of going through life without a lasting intimate love relationship. So when you begin to feel the flutter of those butterflies as your heart approaches the state of love, be wise and advance slowly. Take the time to get to know your new love in every way possible before you decide whether you are infatuated, or really in love. Most importantly, make sure that you are both on the same page in the relationship. Make sure you both have the same understanding of what unconditional love is and what it will take to keep your love alive forever. My personal definition of love follows.

LOVE IS . . .

If I never learn another lesson in my life, it will be all right, because I know I've learned the most important one of all. I've learned what love is and what love is not.

Love is not about reading minds, making assumptions or casting judgments. It's about saying what's on your mind without fear of rejection. Not even a hurtful truth can break the bond you share with the one you love.

Love is not about having expectations about what you can get. It's about not having any expectations at all. It's about having only thoughts of giving and, because of that, you will get what you need too.

Love is not demanding. It is not on a timetable. Love is what it is, when it is, with who it is. Love finds us. We don't find it.

Love is not about being deceptive, hiding your true self or your feelings. It's about baring your soul and knowing that you will be loved no matter what.

Love is not about money or whose bills get paid off first. It's about going through life expecting to be disappointed, because you surely will be.

Love is not about how much sex you have.

Love is not about what you attempt to achieve in life, no matter what the cost.

Love is something you have no control over.

Love is about total acceptance of someone for who they are.

Love is knowing that at the end of each day, you have someone to go home to, someone you trust with all you are or ever will be.

Love is having that special someone look at you everyday with admiration and think that you're beautiful inside and out, always.

Love is never being tempted to lend your heart to another because the one you love is all you've ever wanted, and you know it.

Love is knowing the one you love misses you every minute they're not with you and knowing you fill their day with thoughts of you two together.

Love is holding hands when you watch television together and holding each other close just before dropping off to sleep. You are the first thing your love thinks of when he or she wakes in the morning and his or her last thought at night.

Love is knowing you are the last piece to the puzzle and that you complete him or her in a way no one else ever could.

Love is about trust, truth and forgiveness because your heart will not allow you to do anything else.

Love is a connection to another's soul that cannot and will not ever be broken. Once you have this kind of love, it reigns over your heart forever. This is the only kind of love worth having.

Love is knowing you're the luckiest person alive because of what you have and sometimes because of what you don't have. Love is being grateful for it every day.

Love is about feeling weak in the knees at the thought of touching the one you love. It's about every heartbeat you have.

Love doesn't have to be spoken. Love is about showing someone in a thousand little ways just how much you care.

Love is knowing you could be happy with this person no matter where you live, how much money you have, or how many road blocks life throws in front of you.

Love can't be swayed by others' opinions and can't be measured on any scale.

Love gives you peace and comfort in the quiet moments. It makes you wish you could slow down time, to freeze in those perfect moments when you catch yourself staring at your love, spellbound and overwhelmed.

Love is the calm starry night when your life is a raging storm. It's the voice of reason that talks you down from the cliff you're about to jump off of.

Love is your safety net, and nothing else in the world matters.

Love is having someone who nurtures your soul, feeds your mind and fills up your heart.

Love is powerful, something you never forget, take for granted, or walk away from.

Love is about sharing in the joys and the troubles of the one you love. Love is shared laughter and tears, and adventure. Love is growing old together.

Love makes you want to run into a burning building to save your partner because you don't want to go through life without him or her.

Love is kissing while you wait in line at the grocery store because you don't care who sees you or what they might think.

If you ever have this kind of love and lose it for any reason, may God help you in getting through your loss. If you've never had love like this, believe in it. It does exist. The hard part is making sure, beyond a shadow of doubt, that each partner feels the same way about what love is and what it is not.

9

Dating Again

The next person to capture your heart should be someone who truly knows the value of your spirit. It should be someone who will be willing to do anything to earn your trust and devotion—not just for a little while—but forever. You deserve the very best. Don't ever settle for less.

Always remember, if you have to change the one you're with to be happy or if you feel you need to change yourself to make him or her happy, then you are with the wrong person. Once you decide what you want out of life and how you plan to live it, you must never compromise on these convictions. The standards you set for yourself are not negotiable for anyone.

Finding the Perfect Partner for You

Is your perfect partner still out there? I say, yes. If he or she is not already with you, then they are still out there!

In order to narrow your search, consider making a list of all the qualities you are looking for in a partner. Focus especially on characteristics you have previously compromised—you know, the ones you are no longer willing to negotiate.

Make up a list of questions you need answered to really get to know someone. List things you want your potential partner to know about you. Don't forget important "deal breaker" information which may make them run for the hills or, perhaps, make them like you even more for your convictions.

This is not to suggest that you go right down the list of questions when you meet someone for the first time. But it would be wise to slip at least some of these questions into each conversation you have with the person you are trying to get to know. Do not stop until they are all answered to your satisfaction. And, **do not** accept a date with anyone until you feel comfortable with the answers.

Following is a list of suggested questions to get you started. Remember to add or delete questions as they pertain to your comfort level and lifestyle.

- How many times have you been married? What happened?
- Do you still get along? Any chance of reconciliation?
- How many serious relationships have you had in the last 5 years? What happened?
- Describe your personality.
- What do you want most out of life?
- Describe a typical weekday and weekend for you.
- What are your favorite kinds of music, TV, movies, food, etc.?
- What are your hobbies?
- What kind of education do you have?
- What kinds of jobs have you had? What do you do for a living now?
- Do you live in an apartment or a house? Renting or buying?
- What kind of sports do you like?
- What's the craziest thing you've ever done?
- What's the craziest thing you still want to do?
- What do you do to have fun?
- What's the most romantic thing you've ever done?
- What's the most romantic thing ever done for you?
- Describe your perfect mate.
- Do you have any children? Where do they live? How old are they?

- Why do you think someone should be attracted to you?
- What are your good qualities? What's not so good about you?
- How do you feel about drinking, smoking, and drugs?
- How do you feel about sex?
- What are your talents?
- Describe your perfect first, second and third date.
- How do you think dating is supposed to go now?
- What turns you on? What turns you off?
- How is your health? Are you on any medications? For what?
- Tell me about your family.
- What is your religious background?
- What are your views on honesty and fidelity?
- Have you ever been cheated on?
- Have you ever cheated on someone? Why?
- Do you think marriage and the vows are outdated?
- Why is it so hard for some people to stay monogamous?

Whatever list you create should be flexible—except for your non-negotiable items, of course. You will need to compromise on some things because no one is perfect, as you know. But the right person is worth small compromises. Keep in mind that your future mate will have a mental list of his own that he will, no doubt, also need to compromise on.

When the Relationship Deepens

Before two people decide to commit to a relationship, especially marriage, they should be serious enough to search their hearts, minds and souls. When they are prepared to go to this level, they can each ask the deeper, more intimate questions, as follows:

- Can I spend the rest of my life with this person?
- Do I love this person unconditionally despite any faults he or she has now or may have in the future?
- Will I be happy with this person without wanting to cheat on him or her later?
- Can I trust this person to mean and keep the promises he or she makes?
- Can I trust him or her to not hurt me?

All answers must be yes or the relationship is bound to fail. If you are really determined to have a committed relationship, take the time to get the answers.

Desirable Qualities

Most men and women would agree, the following qualities should be considered when searching for a potential mate:

- Someone with a life defined by morality, honesty and integrity.
- Someone with a good and beautiful soul you can love.
- Someone with intelligence, grace and a healthy sense of humor you can appreciate.
- Someone with a kind and thoughtful heart speaking silently to yours.
- Someone with a life prioritized appropriately.
- Someone with an easy going and patient demeanor and slow to anger.
- Someone you can admire for his or her hard work ethic and financial stability.
- Someone you can trust to catch you when you stumble.
- Someone who is romantic and sentimental with whom you can be excited to be around.
- Someone mom and the kids will like.
- Someone with vision and dreams you can share.
- Someone you will have similar interests with.
- Someone who is independent, as well as emotionally and financially secure.

Some of these qualities may not be important to you. This list is merely meant to give you a few ideas when compiling your own list.

Where to Go, What to Look For

Go slowly and be careful as you venture back out into the dating world. You might still be very vulnerable, and therefore, easily taken advantage of. With this in mind, it's probably time to take full advantage of the many available resources to meet people of character. You have literally hundreds of options to explore in meeting new people. Some suggestions follow:

Social Clubs and Community Events

There are likely a wide variety of clubs in your area where you can meet local men and women with some of your same interests. If you like gardening, check into a garden club. If you like to golf or play tennis or swim, join the country club. If you're more into business, try the chamber of commerce.

Picking Up The Pieces

Join a health club. Go to a coffeehouse or bookstore and strike up a conversation. Attend outdoor events advertised on radio or in your newspaper.

Try your church. For the active churchgoer, this should be the first place to look.

Nightclubs

Go to nightclubs and have a ball dancing the night away. These days, women dance by themselves even if they don't know anyone. Men usually take notice that you're by yourself and will often ask you to dance with them.

Blind Dates

Go on a blind date set up by a close friend who knows your likes and dislikes.

Parties

Attend parties or throw some yourself. Encourage your guests to bring a new friend for you to meet.

Internet Dating Services

The Internet provides many options for singles. From simple chat rooms to dating services, the Internet is sure to fit your needs in some area. At the very least, you can do a lot of research by computer. If you don't have access to the Internet, ask a friend to help you.

Search on-line at one of the many Internet "matchmaker" services. Many are free, anonymous, and fun. These services allow you to set very specific criteria for what kind of person would be a good match for you. After their database searches for the qualities you are looking for, they e-mail you with potential matches. After reviewing the match profiles, you can decide if you want to contact anyone, if at all. It's entirely up to you. Post a profile of yourself with a picture and see what happens.

Speed Dating

This face-to-face method of meeting many eligible people in one place is a hot trend now. There are many speed dating sites on the Internet that host speed dates all over the country. It is usually free to become a member and from there, you can reserve a paid spot on the next speed date in your area. At the event, you should be able to meet anywhere from 15 to 25 people by sitting with each participant for 4 to 6 minutes. The dates are segmented in different ways, from age group to race and cultural preference. The dates are usually held in a designated room in a local restaurant. Speed dating costs about $35 per session and it's safe, easy and cost effective. Every participant has a vested interest in meeting you. Everyone is there for the same reason.

If you meet someone you think may be compatible with you, I suggest you start out as just friends. Talk to him or her on the phone a lot and try to get to know them before inviting them to your home or into your life. Subtly review the questions found at the beginning of this chapter. Last, take your time. Be patient for the right person.

First Dates:
Do's and Don'ts for the Clueless

Still think you might be a one-hit wonder when it comes to getting dates? You may be one of thousands of clueless singles with a below par batting average. Make every date a home run with these easy do's and don'ts for first dates. Keep in mind, first dates are your time to shine and show off your charming personality. This is your chance to make a lasting impression. Do it with savvy and verve. Good luck guys and girls.

To DO List for Clueless Guys:

- DO put as much time into getting ready for your date as she will. You should be freshly showered, have fresh breath, and smell fantastic! You should be well groomed as well, meaning that any facial hair such as eyebrows, nose hair and beard should be trimmed.

- Do make sure your fingernails and toenails are clean and manicured. You will feel like a million bucks and your date will take notice.

- DO bring a single flower or some token with you for your date.

- DO open doors and pull out chairs for your date.

- DO call her if you say you will.

- DO treat your date as if she is the last woman on earth. Devotion is intoxicating and very sexy.

123

- DO take her to a place where you can both relax and talk. Consider adding an activity or humor to the date. Research shows that activity and humor produce more successful dates.

- DO be prepared for anything from slaying ex-dragons to fixing a flat tire.

- DO take enough money with you to cover the date and tips.

- DO be observant and considerate. If she is cold, offer her your jacket. If her eyes are glazing over, change the topic of conversation. If she appears tired, cut the date short so she can get some rest.

To DO List for Clueless Girls:

- DO dress appropriately for your date. If going on a picnic or to the races, heels and a skirt are not wise.

- DO take money and a cell phone with you just in case your date turns out to be a jerk. You may get stuck with dinner and a cab ride home.

- DO tell someone where you are going and with whom. You never know when that information will come in handy.

- DO give your date a few choices to choose from when asked where you would like to go or what you would like to do. Men love it when a woman can make a decision.

- DO unlock the driver side car door if your date is kind enough to open your door first.

To DO List for Both Guys & Girls:

- DO be on time.

- DO listen intently to what your date has to say. Your date is giving you a wealth of information you can use later.

- DO be open and honest about yourself.

- DO find out what you both have in common and build on that.

- DO be yourself.

- DO flirt with your date.

- DO have fun.

- DO ask questions about your date, and his or her interests. Doing so will exhibit your desire to learn more about your date and this will make them feel special.

- DO answer ALL questions asked of you, one at a time and completely. Evasiveness or your inattention to detail may turn off your date. They will also grow tired of having to drag conversation out of you.

- DO share your feelings on what you are passionate about with your date. These things tell a lot about a person.

- DO compliment your date on his or her positive qualities and thank your date for making the effort to get to know you better.

- DO smile. This could be the beginning of something extraordinary. If it turns out not to be…. then, at least you got out of the house.

The DON'T List for Clueless Guys:

- DON'T pick your date up in a filthy car, inside or out.

- DON'T use coupons for dinner. Save them for yourself.

- DON'T crack one thousand jokes. She will not appreciate your corny humor.

- DON'T talk non-stop about yourself. She wants to like you on her own without being "sold" on you by you.

- DON'T drink too much. You are driving.

- DON'T take advantage of her if she drinks too much.

- DON'T use profanity, belch, or scratch your private parts unless your date does too. Only those that do don't mind if others do too.

- DON'T date at all if you expect sex as repayment for dinner. She is doing you the favor by going out with you.

The DON'T List for Clueless Girls:

- DON'T order the most expensive thing on the menu unless you are prepared to pay for it, if the need arises.

- DON'T drink too much.

The DON'T List for Both Guys & Girls:

- DON'T interrupt your date while he or she is speaking. This is a key sign that you are not listening.

- DON'T talk about things you know nothing about or use words for which you do not know the true meaning.

- DON'T talk about your ex unless asked. Even then, make it brief enough to answer the question.

- DON'T complain about anything. Not about your life, your job, your ex, etc. Always be positive.

When Should You Become Intimate?

Some couples decide early on to explore the physical side of a relationship. Only you can be the judge of when the time is right. Historically speaking, having sex before one really knows their partner usually proves to be an empty attempt at making a connection. If a connection is made, it may be fleeting at best. For many however, a connection is neither required nor expected in order to be intimate. This is fine as long as the feeling is mutual. Whenever intimacy becomes part of the picture, DO be safe about it.

Second Date Checklist:

Use this checklist if you are considering going out with a person for the second or third time. If you answer YES to the following questions, then you should have a great second and third date.

- Did you have a good time?
- Did you laugh?

- Did you have good conversation and communicate well?
- Are you attracted to the way your date looks?
- Would your first date rate a 7 or higher?
- Are you attracted to your date's personality?
- Were you treated well and with respect?
- Does your date seem to be straightforward with nothing to hide?
- Does your date exhibit qualities you are looking for in a partner?

Red Flags

Following are some types of individuals and situations you may want to be wary of. These are situations that should sound off bells and whistles in your mind.

Temporary Representatives

Many people are experts at being one person when you meet them and later turning into someone completely unrelated. Make sure you are getting to know the real person, not just their temporary representative.

The representative is the person who is always charming, romantic, considerate, loving, and trustworthy.

This representative always knows what to say and just when to say it. He or she represents all the qualities you have revealed that you are looking for in a permanent mate.

If the representatives are really good at what they do, you will fall in love with them only to find out later (usually too late) that they have finally untied the real guy or girl who was being held in the back room, bound and gagged. The representative then disappears, never to be heard from again.

If the real guy or girl needed a representative, you can imagine what he or she is probably really like. In short, make sure the person you are dating is a good enough, real enough person, and he or she doesn't need a representative. Again, you can save a lot of heartache by taking any new relationship slowly and by asking a lot of varied questions. Seeing a person in many different social situations and meeting and talking with their friends can reveal character inconsistencies as well.

Never Married By Their Mid-Forties

Beware of men or women who are in their mid-forties and have never been married or had any long lasting relationships to speak of. Many of these folks have never owned a house, have no furniture, a low-rent car, no true career and nothing much to show for their lives. I know from painful experience that some of these people don't manage money well. One reason they lack some of these items may be that some move from relationship to relationship, never staying in one place long enough to accumulate any worthwhile possessions. If they do have any, chances are their partner provided them. Many of these folks want a committed relationship, but are a little too picky. After all, no one is perfect. Many of these folks can be hard to live with and some have trouble making long term commitments.

In all fairness though, there are of course exceptions to every rule. Today, many men and women are busy making something of their lives in the form of obtaining a higher education or building their careers before settling down. Many forty-something singles simply love the single life and feel just as complete single as they would feel married. Many of these folks have the best personalities in the world with wonderful hearts. They have simply not met the right person and are unwilling to settle for less, nor should they. All I'm saying is be careful and go with your gut.

Self-centeredness

People who talk only about themselves are one of two things. Either they are so desperate to connect with someone that they begin to shamelessly "sell" themselves, or they simply don't care to know anything about you.

All flash and no substance

If you are female, beware of the guy with the perfect nose, who has a handsome face and possesses the sculpted body of Adonis. He has perfect teeth, beautiful eyes and smile to match. If you are male, beware of the woman with the perfect hair, manicured nails and figure to die for.

We all have imperfections. Don't forget that. Do remember this—their imperfections are not visible. Make sure this person is actually willing to communicate with you on an intelligent level. When you reach your golden years, conversation may be all you have left. Unfortunately, it has been my experience that many people like this are all show and depend highly on their looks to get through life.

You may find yourself having to drag out every answer to your questions. The type of person to watch out for is the one who usually speaks in three-word sentences because they are very poor communicators. You will soon tire of making all the effort in trying to communicate with this type of person.

Promptness

Observe the promptness of the person you are considering dating. I happen to believe there is a direct correlation between a person's promptness, or lack thereof, to how well they keep their promises.

If someone is always early, I deem this person to be highly dependable, even eager. If someone is promptly on time, he or she is also dependable and means what they say. If someone is always running 15 minutes late, you're on his or her list but you're not at the top. Still we all have our flaws and tardiness could simply mean poor time management. Watch out for the person who is always an hour or more late. For this one, you are definitely not a priority.

If your radar is off, let someone else's gut be your guide when selecting a partner. Choose someone who knows you extremely well and who is a good judge of character to be your guide. This adviser would also be someone who would not be as easily swayed by the charms your new friend may possess.

Conclusion

Do you still love the one that broke your heart? Don't worry if the answer is yes. It is okay to feel that way, even though you may never be a couple again.

You should give yourself permission to feel any way that will get you through recovery. I still cherish the love my husband and I used to share, but I no longer cherish the man. He is not the same person I fell in love with.

Are you better off without your partner? Only you can answer that question, but if the answer is yes, don't dwell on the past. Focus on the present and what the future might bring.

Make yourself happy. Be grateful that you no longer have someone in your life that doesn't love and respect you.

Will you find true and lasting love? There's no doubt in my mind that you can. Look forward to that day with great hope and anticipation. There's no greater feeling on earth than that of new love. New love, if it's right, turns into true love. Be ready!

I've picked up the pieces and I'm whole again. And you will be too.

Your Heartbreak Survivor's Resource Guide

The following is a list of available resources for anyone coping with the stressful effects of an emotional breakup. I have included such topics as budgeting money and managing stress and much more. These resources have always been available to you, but you might not have thought to check them out when you were part of a couple.

You *do* need to manage these parts of your life, whether you know how to or not. I feel it is imperative that we all take a realistic look at our resources and build upon them. I sincerely hope this guide will be helpful to all who use it.

Managing and Budgeting Your Money

When coping with the stressful effects of an emotional breakup, finances are usually pretty low on the priority

list. Unfortunately, the urgent need to manage and budget
money will never be more key to your survival than right
now. Here is an easy to follow guide to managing and
budgeting your money.

The first thing you want to do is take a realistic look at
your financial obligations. Start by writing down the names
of your creditors and the payment amounts, then sort these
by due date.

Next, decide what amounts can be paid with each
paycheck. For example: For those who are paid on the 1st
and the 15th of the month, you must pay the bills due by
the 15th with the paycheck you received on the 1st. Always
pay your bills early. The alternative is paying late fees and
earning bad credit, which will hurt you more than you can
imagine.

Bills due around the 15th (use paycheck from 1st)

Creditor	$_____
Creditor	$_____
Creditor	$_____
Food (for 2 weeks)	$_____
Gasoline(for 2 weeks)	$_____
Daycare (for 2 weeks)	$_____
Car Ins.	$_____
Electric	$_____

Misc.	$_____
Cash	$_____
Total	$_____

Bills due around the 1ˢᵗ (use paycheck from 15ᵗʰ)

Creditor	$_____
Creditor	$_____
Creditor	$_____
Food (for 2 weeks)	$_____
Gasoline(for 2 weeks)	$_____
Daycare (for 2 weeks)	$_____
Rent	$_____
Phone	$_____
Cable	$_____
Misc.	$_____
Cash	$_____
Total	$_____

Now, list all income received by the 1ˢᵗ, then subtract the amount you must pay out by the 1ˢᵗ. Do the same thing for income received by the 15ᵗʰ.

If the ending figure is negative, then you need to figure out where the remaining needed money will come from.

Ideas for Extra Income

If you fall short during the month you must make up the difference. Here are some ideas for generating extra income. Take a part-time job with flexible hours. Or, create your own job. Start by running an ad in the newspaper and do any number of small jobs. Do weekend house cleaning. Type research papers or dissertations for college students. Baby-sit children during highly desirable, off-hours for parents who do shift work.

Consider selling corporate gift baskets to local companies. Maintain employee birthday, anniversary, and promotions lists, and set up a contract of sorts to service these companies year round.

If you have a spare room in your house, rent it out to someone. Make sure you carefully investigate any potential boarder's background beforehand.

There are any number of things you can do to earn extra cash. Ask your family and friends for suggestions.

A Few Last Tips

- Learn to buy only what you need.
- Don't live on your credit cards. The best option is to pay cash. This way, if you can't afford it, you won't buy it.
- Buy as many generic products as possible.

- Make sure you always leave enough money in your account for unexpected expenses, like car repairs, school supplies, etc.
- Discontinue luxury services such as cable or satellite TV, lawn care, long-distance phone calls, cellular phones or pagers, manicures, etc.
- No matter how much it hurts, try to save $10 a week. That may not sound like much, but you may find yourself living off your piggy bank someday.

Managing Your Stress

When coping with the stressful effects of an emotional breakup, managing stress and finding support are paramount to successful recovery. Here is an easy to follow guide to help you over the rough spots.

Imagine for a moment that your best friend has all the same stress that you do. This is the kind of friend you would do absolutely anything for. You want only happiness for her and permanent relief from her stress.

The objective here is to remove yourself from your own stress and to make it someone else's so that you can analyze it more objectively.

The first step is to itemize your friend's reasons for stress. Then, itemize why your friend is currently unable to manage this stress. Next, review the reasons for the stress and categorize them into the following areas of stress:

- Finances / Job
- Love and Relationships
- Home
- Health
- Children and Family

Once categorized, take each category, one at a time, and list three possible ways to manage each item and the possible outcomes. Then highlight the safest, most realistic way for your friend to achieve the desired outcome. When done, step back and look at the steps you have recommended for your friend to take.

Take each highlighted recommendation and list the possible obstacles or roadblocks that may prevent your friend from completing this step. Then, next to each obstacle, list the best and quickest way it can be neutralized.

Turn the stress back over to yourself now and tackle these stress categories one at a time. Deal with them one by one because each one will require 100 percent of your focus. Once you are satisfied that a particular stress is under control and you are taking the steps to manage it, move on to the next category.

The following serves as a working guide for managing stress.

Reason for Stress: Long divorce proceedings.

You are Unable to Manage this Stress Because:
You are financially overwhelmed.

Category of Stress: Finance

3 Ways to Manage the Stress:
1. Commit to a budget.
2. Increase income either through current job or additional job.
3. Make a financial plan and stick to it.

Possible Outcome:
1. This is a good idea, but will not change the current financial picture much.
2. This will lessen the financial burden.
3. This will give direction, but will not lessen the burden.

Recommendation: Option 2 is best for immediate results. Recommend incorporating with option 1 and 3.

Roadblocks to Recommendation: Fatigue

Best Way to Neutralize the Roadblock:
1. Remember the need to work more hours is only temporary.
2. Realize it has to be done to reduce your stress.
3. Rearrange your schedule to get enough rest to avoid fatigue.

With nothing standing in your way, you have no other choice but to succeed. If you have a sound plan, and you work that plan, you will be successful. God Bless and Good Luck!

*Note: There are many prescription drugs on the market today for relief of anxiety. A professional can prescribe one right for you.

Visit My Web Site

Visit www.mattersoflove.com where you can join as a member. It's free. You will find everything you need for the heart—from all things romantic for new love to first aid for the broken heart. You can submit requests for advice. You can also submit or view poetry, photographs, and tips for great romantic adventures. You can even contribute to my future relationship books. You can search for Heartbreak Survival Workshop locations and locate support group sponsors in your area. You will also enjoy a multitude of excellent links and resources. In the future, many relationship and self-help articles and newsletters will be featured.

Join Support Groups

If you do only one thing for yourself after a breakup, find or create a support group. Having encouragement makes a world of difference in your recovery time. At the same time, you can be a support to someone else.

Create Your Own Group

Custom-build a network of experience and help for yourself and others by creating your own women's or men's group. You may find this is a very rewarding part of your life.

Gather your support group together and give it a name. Elect a president, vice-president, secretary, treasurer and sergeant at arms. Formulate your mission as a group. Decide when and where to meet and what member dues will be. From there, what you do with your group is up to you. Here are a few suggestions.

- Perform community service for women, children or the elderly.
- Have guest speakers talk about issues of interest.

- Prepare covered dishes once a month at alternating houses.
- Go on group outings to the movies, amusement parks, or go camping.
- Help each other with minor home repairs.
- Host "speed dating" or singles parties.

Once a month, select from your group a "Queen or King for the Day". For that person, the group volunteers to clean the house, wash the car, cook dinner, and bring a small gift. All of these things are great fun for everyone, and each member gets their own time to be pampered and made to feel special.

The benefits of creating a support group are limitless. You can give and receive advice, talk with your peers, make new friends, increase your ability to socialize, and explore new activities and interests.

You can even share resources within the group. For example, trade off on baby-sitting so that your members can have some quiet time or go out on a date.

If you have limited friends and family, sign in at www. mattersoflove.com and select the Support Group section. I am continually building a list of people in your area who would like to start or join a support group.

Recommended Books

*A Woman's Guide to Healing
the Heartache of Divorce,* by Rose Sweet

When He Leaves, by Kari West and Noelle Quinn

Rebuilding: When Your Relationship Ends, by
Bruce Fisher, Robert E. Alberti and Virginia M. Satir

Master Dating: How to Meet & Attract Quality Men, by
Felicia Rose Adler and Angela C. Fernandez

Soul Dating to Soul Mating, by Basha Kaplan

Music to Soothe the Soul

Love Songs—David Sanbourne

Ocean surf/ Sounds of Everglades/ Golden Pond—
Relax With

Sailboat Journey/ Song of Whales/ Ocean Surf—
Relax With

Nature Sounds— Growing Minds with Music

Community Services

For legal advice, Social Services, grief counseling, and self-help support groups consult the front of your local phone book. Look under Community Services. I encourage you to use these services to get whatever assistance you may need.

Inspirational
Notes & Quotes

One cannot get through life without pain.
What we can do is choose how to use
the pain life presents to us.
Bernie Seigel

Not everything that is faced can be changed,
but nothing can be changed until it is faced.
James Baldwin

We learn to fly not by becoming fearless,
but by the daily practice of courage.
Sam Keen

Wealth lost—something lost;
honor lost—much lost; Courage lost—all lost.
German proverb

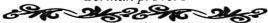

Dreams are…illustrations from the book
your soul is writing about you.
Marsha Norman

Hold fast to dreams, for if dreams die,
life is a broken-winged bird
that cannot fly.
Langston Hughes

Faith is the strength
by which a shattered world
shall emerge into light.
Helen Keller

Faith is confirmed by the heart,
confessed by the tongue,
and acted upon by the body.
Sufi Proverb

The strength of the heart
comes from the soundness of the faith.
Arabian Proverb

The art of living lies less in eliminating our troubles
than in growing with them.
Bernard M. Baruch

It is good to have an end to journey toward,
but it is the journey that matters in the end.
Ursula K. LeGuin

You can only go halfway into the forest;
then you are coming out the other side.
Chinese Proverb

Life is what happens
when you're making other plans.
John Lennon

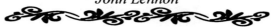

If you don't know where you are going,
how can you expect to get there?
Basil S. Walsh

Optimism is the cheerful frame of mind
that enables a teakettle to sing,
though in hot water up to its nose.
Harold Helfer

Looking for peace is like looking
for a turtle with a mustache:
you won't be able to find it.
but when your heart is ready,
peace will come looking for you.
Ajahn Chah

Once we learn to touch peace, we will be healed
and transformed. It is not a matter of faith;
it is a matter of practice.
Thich Nhat Hanh

The best way out is always through.
Robert Frost

The man who removes a mountain
begins by
carrying away small stones.
Chinese Proverb

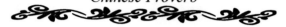

Life can only be understood backwards;
but it must be lived forwards.
Soren Kierkegaard

Every day is a new life. Seize it. Live it.
David Guy Powers

New seed is faithful. It roots deepest
in the places that are most empty.
Clarissa Pinkola Estes

To live fully is to let go and die with
each passing moment,
and to be reborn in each new one.
Jack Kornfield

Inside myself is a place where I live alone
and that's where you renew your springs
that never dry up.
Pearl Buck

It isn't until you come to a spiritual understanding of who
you are—not necessarily a religious feeling,
but deep down, the spirit within—
that you can begin to take control.
Oprah Winfrey

The art of true healing is
when you can stimulate
a person's own spirit to shine through.
Sandra Ingerman

Trust life, and it will teach you,
in joy and sorrow,
all you need to know.
James Baldwin

It always comes back to the same necessity: go deep
enough and there is a bedrock of truth,
however hard.
May Sarton

Each of us has a remarkable capacity
for self-healing.
However, we have to be the ones to tap it.
Stephan Rechtschaffen

To wish to be well is part of becoming well.
Seneca

Inside yourself or outside,
you never have to change what you see,
only the way you see it.
Thaddeus Goals

Love is patient and kind: it is not jealous or conceited or
proud: love is not ill mannered or selfish or irritable:
love does not keep a record of wrongs;
love is not happy with evil,
but is happy with the truth.
Love never gives up;
and its faith, hope and patience never fail.
Corinthians 1   13:4-7

There are two fatal errors
that keep great projects from coming to life:
1. Not finishing
2. Not starting
Buddha

Love is stronger than pride.
Author unknown

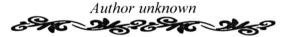

Security is mostly a superstition. It does not exist in nature, nor do the children of men as a whole experience it. Avoiding danger is no safer in the long run than outright exposure. Life is either a daring adventure, or nothing.
Helen Keller

In every woman there is a queen.
Speak to the queen and the queen will answer.
Norwegian Proverb

The secret of getting ahead is getting started.
The secret to getting started is breaking your complex,
overwhelming tasks into small manageable tasks,
and then starting on the first one.
Mark Twain

It's amazing what God can do with a
broken heart when given all the pieces.
Anonymous

While we have the gift of life,
it seems to me the only tragedy
is to allow part of us to die—
whether it is our spirit,
our creativity or our glorious uniqueness.
Gilda Radner

Even if you're on the right track,
you'll get run over if you just sit there.
Will Rogers

A chief gave his son a beautiful crystal on the advent
of his becoming a man. The chief held the stone to the
light and as he did the light shone through it and a
spectrum of colors lit the room. He said, " behold my
son, it is the flaws in the stone that allow the colors to
shine through. And so it is with life".
Native American Fable

165

Picking Up The Pieces

I found the following beautiful writing in Sylvia Browne's book, *A Psychic's Guide to Our World and Beyond—The Other Side and Back.*

THE INVITATION
Oriah Mountain Dreamer,
Indian Elder

It doesn't interest me what you do for a living. I want to know what you ache for, and if you dare to dream of meeting your heart's longing.

It doesn't interest me how old you are. I want to know if you will risk looking a fool for love, for your dreams, for the adventure of being alive.

It doesn't interest me what planets are squaring your moon. I want to know if you have touched the center of your own sorrow, if you have been opened by life's betrayals or have become shriveled and closed from fear of further pain.

I want to know if you can sit with pain, mine or your own, without moving to hide it or fade it or fix it.

I want to know if you can be with joy, mine or your own, if you can dance with wildness and let the ecstasy fill you to the tips of your fingers and toes without cautioning us to be careful, to be realistic, to remember the limitations of being human.

It doesn't interest me if the story you are telling me is true. I want to know if you can disappoint another to be true to yourself; if you can bear the accusation of betrayal and not betray your own soul, if you can be faithless and therefore be trustworthy.

I want to know if you can see beauty, even when it's not pretty, every day, and if you can source your own life from its presence.

I want to know if you can live with failure, yours and mine, and still stand on the edge of a lake and shout to the silver moon, "Yes"!

It doesn't interest me to know where you live or how much money you have. I want to know if you can get up, after the night of grief and despair, weary and bruised to the bone, and do what needs to be done to feed the children.

It doesn't interest me who you know or how you came to be here. I want to know if you will stand in the center of the fire with me and not shrink back.

It doesn't interest me where or what or with whom you have studied. I want to know what sustains you, from the inside, when all else falls away.

I want to know if you can be alone with yourself and if you truly like the company you keep in the empty moments.

You can do anything you want to,
if you are determined enough.

Only you are responsible for your happiness.
What are you doing about it?

You are a beautiful person with a lot to offer.
You deserve the very best.
Don't ever accept less.

If you don't respect yourself,
no one else will either.

If you depend only on yourself,
you will never be disappointed.

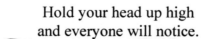

Hold your head up high
and everyone will notice.

The only one worth your tears
is the one who cries with you.
If the one you love isn't out there crying,
then you shouldn't be either.

Wondering how you're going to make it through
another day? Well, you have to make it, because
if you don't, your ex wins.
Don't give anyone that power!

Remember to breathe today.
Your heart needs the oxygen!

You are the only one who can change what's wrong in your life and protect what's right about it.

Make a conscious decision, a promise to yourself,
to surround yourself with positive people.
You no longer have the time, energy or inclination
to be with any other type of person.

Today is what you make it. Make it a great one.

What you do today paves your future.

Do something nice for yourself today.
You deserve it.

Do something nice for someone else.
It's nice to be appreciated.

Remember why you were happy
before you met your ex.
You can get back to that place again.
Focus on it.

Know that you're going to be ok.
In order to get there, though, you have to let yourself.

Focus on forgetting old memories.
Take steps to create new and wonderful ones
with those in your life now.
You'll be surprised how just little happy moments will help
you now and in the future.

Starting now, try to make one new friend a month.
At the end of the year,
you'll have twelve great new friends!

You have the power to shape your future any way you like.
Don't dwell on a past you can't change.

.

The more you think of yourself,
the less you will think of your ex.

If you find yourself thinking of your ex,
ask yourself if he or she is thinking of you.
If the answer is no,
focus on something more important.

Cherish every day. Every day you get a chance to start over
and make things right in your life.
Don't waste it.

Attitude is everything.
If you think it's going to be a great day, it will be.

Assess what you have lost…Time from your life and memories that are now only meaningful to you. You've also lost someone who breaks promises, lies and cheats. He's not such a big loss after all.

Don't ever be ashamed for loving someone,
even the wrong someone.
Love is the purest emotion we have.
It's the emotion we have the least control over. Many people go through life, blind to what love feels like or how to recognize opportunities for love.
Your next love could be delivering your mail, repairing your car, teaching your child, or living right next door.
Keep your heart, your mind and your eyes open.

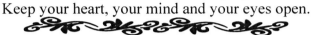

Remember—if you are not with the one you love
because he or she left,
then your ex was never yours completely.
A fully committed heart never leaves.
No other type of love is acceptable.

Never give up on yourself.

POP GOES THE WEASEL.
God, I hope so.

Never, ever stop trying to be happy.
If you do, only you will lose.
Its time for you to win the life you deserve.

Someone recently commented on what a survivor I am.
When faced with the alternative,
I realize I never have any other choice.

The day you forgive your ex is the day you set yourself free
from the power he or she held over you,
and the sorrow caused within you.

On a scale of 1 to 10, you are a 40.
He left you for a 2, which makes him a zero.

You can't push the boulder up the mountain
by yourself.

You can't hold back the ocean,
so you must learn how to swim.

If your dream is to live in a house,
don't settle for an apartment.

Don't "discount" yourself
by dating a "marked down" person.

BIBLIOGRAPHY

Goldman, Caren. Healing Words for the Body, Mind and Spirit. New York: Marlow & Company, 2001.

Browne, Sylvia, with Lindsay Harrison. The Other Side and Back: A Psychic's Guide to Our World and Beyond. New York: Signet, 2000.

Good News Bible: Today's English Version. New York: American Bible Society, 1976.

Webster's Seventh New Collegiate Dictionary: Massachusetts: G. & C. Merriam Company,1979.

Gilda Radner Page. "Quote Me On It…" 4 July 2003 <http://www.quotemeonit.com/radner.html>

Proverbs from Norway Page. Creative Proverbs. 4 July 2003 <http://creativeproverbs.com/no01. htm>

Hellen Keller Quotes Page. The Quotations Page. 4 July 2003 <http://www.quotationspage.com/ Quotes/Hellen_Keller/11>

Will Rogers Page. Quoteland. 4 July 2003 <http:// www.quoteland.com/author.asp?AUTHOR_ID=18>

Collected Quotations Page. Science of Mind Foundation. 1 December, 2001 <http://www. Somfoundation.org/somfpage36.html>

Afterword

When I set out to write this book, my intention was to make sure that no other person on earth would have to learn how to pick up the pieces—all alone. By trial and error, I found my way back from the darkness and vowed to share the recovery steps that work with all that need them.

If you enjoyed the book and would like to ensure that many others are made aware of it's merits, then please review it. Take a moment to go on-line to the bookstores listed below and review Picking Up The Pieces: A Guide to Recovery from Betrayal and a Broken Heart by Dinah S. Temple.

http://www.amazon.com
http://www.barnes&noble.com
http://www.booksamillion.com

On the home page, use the search box to search for the book category and type in Dinah S. Temple. Then click GO. Click on the appropriate book. When the book information comes up, click Customer Reviews. You may enter your own review at that time.

My heart and thoughts are with each one of you as you pick up the pieces of your own broken heart. Thanks for your support. Be well and happy!

Love,
Dinah

ABOUT THE AUTHOR

Dinah S. Temple holds a Bachelor of Science Degree in Business Administration from Virginia Commonwealth University. Ms. Temple is currently working on two new books. She writes from her home in Colonial Heights, Virginia and conducts Heartbreak Survival Workshops by request. Ms. Temple owns and runs the web site www.mattersoflove.com, which was designed with broken hearts in mind. The web site provides information on support groups, her books, relationship advice, as well as heartbreak survival workshops and much more. Ms. Temple is also the Relationships Editor for the women's on-line community group Bellaonline, which can be found on the Internet at www.bellaonline.com.

Ms. Temple actively writes relationship articles and newsletters for Bellaonline and other web sites.

Printed in the United States
68652LVS00001B/62

9 781418 440473